# Practical
# Remote Team
# Leadership

## Methods, Tools and Templates for Virtual Leaders

Emanuela Giangregorio

2nd Edition

# Copyright

# Practical Remote Team Leadership

First Edition Published in 2016

**Author**: Emanuela Giangregorio

## Other Books by this Author

Practical Project Management

Practical Project Stakeholder Management

# Acknowledgements

I have learnt most of what I know about leading remote teams and working effectively in virtual teams from my experience working with my clients over the last 20 years. I thank everyone that has given me an opportunity to lead a project, coach you, train your teams or consult to your organisation.

I also wish to thank all my readers and appreciate your complements. Some of you have invited me into your organisations to deliver training and team building for your teams – fantastic experiences, thank you!

Emanuela Giangregorio,
Performance Improvement Coach

# Contents

# 1| Introduction

*"I can resist everything except temptation."*

-Oscar Wilde

I have been tempted to write this book for ages, and finally it reached the top of my priority list. In recent years, the most popular topic I have been asked to consult and train on is how to lead remote teams effectively. This is not a new subject area, as distributed teams have been the norm in most organisations for over 20 years. Many books have also been written on leading remote teams, so why this book?

The feedback I've had from people attending my courses is that they have read several books on remote team management and leadership, but they have found very few practical take-aways that they could implement immediately. Most of these people are senior managers who don't have time to devise their own tools and templates. They want tangible, practical guidance to help them in their roles. That is what this book provides. A toolkit to help you manage and lead remote teams effectively.

I do not dwell on the challenges associated with leading remotely. I expect the reason you purchased this book is because you are all too familiar with the challenges and want insights on how to overcome them.

## Tools and Templates for You to Use

I have provided a number of tools and templates in this book, including some worked examples where relevant. If you are skim-reading through the book just to see the templates, look for this symbol:

### List of Tools and Templates

1. 5 Benefits Evaluation Scorecard
2. 7 Benefits Evaluation Scorecard - Weighted
3. Remote Leadership Complexity Assessment
4. Code of Collaboration Example
5. Remote Team Effectiveness Assessment
6. RACI and PARIS Matrix
7. 1:1 DASH Meeting Framework
8. Team Performance Dashboards
9. Individual Task List for Matrix Managers
10. Team Motivation Needs
11. PLANTT Communication Checklist
12. Meeting Effort-Value Audit
13. PASTA Virtual Meeting Checklist
14. CARE Email Checklist
15. Email Protocol Example
16. Checklist: Attributes of the Ideal Remote Team Member
17. Remote Team Member Interview Sheet

## Some Important Definitions

1. **Co-located**: A team member is **co-located** with their leader if their leader is in the same office as they are. Likewise, an entire team is **co-located** if the members all work in the same office location.

2. **Remote**: A team member is **remote from their leader** if they work at a different location from their leader.

3. **Distributed**: A team is **distributed** if the members each work in different locations around the country or in different countries.

4. **Virtual**: A team is **virtual** if their primary means of interaction is by using technology, and they hardly or never meet face-to-face.

5. **Gender:** I use "him" to refer to both genders when speaking generally unless referring to a specific example of a person where I will refer to the relevant gender.

6. **Manager** vs **Leader**: When I refer to a "manager", I mean the person/team's line manager. When I refer to "leader", this person may or may not be the team member's line manager, e.g. Project Team Leaders.

7. **Matrix organisation structure**: Many remote team managers and leaders find themselves operating in a matrix organisation structure. The reporting relationships are set up as a grid, or *matrix*, rather than in a traditional hierarchical organisation structure. As a matrix manager, I could have people in my team for whom I have line management responsibility *and also* have people reporting to me functionally, but they have

their own line managers. Some remote team leaders could have no line management responsibility – all their team members report to them indirectly in a matrix organisation structure.


oooOooo

# 2| Key Benefits of Distributed Teaming

*"Strategic thinking is about how you connect the dots."*

-Richard Bandler

**Tools and Templates in this Chapter:**

- 5 Benefits Evaluation Scorecard

- 7 Benefits Evaluation Scorecard - Weighted

In the yin and yang of life there are as many benefits to establishing teams in other regions as there are challenges in working with a distributed team. However, if one weighs up the benefits and challenges, it certainly is more beneficial *overall* for most organisations to work within a regionally distributed organisation structure.

From time to time, I am asked by small and medium size enterprises (SMEs) to evaluate their business and determine whether they would benefit from establishing a business presence in other territories – nationally or internationally. I use a simple scorecard that I developed based on what I believe are the top five benefits for expanding, or restructuring, to have a presence in geographically distributed regions. On the back of that assessment, I would develop a thorough investment appraisal looking at the 3-, 5- or 10-year costs associated with regionalising, and the quantifiable benefits over the same period.

## Top 5 Benefits of Distributed Teaming

### 1. Increase Sales

Your organisation exists to make money. Even if it is a not-for-profit/charity organisation, it still has to make money. Therefore, one of the key benefits should be to increase income, which I refer to in my scorecard as sales.

Having team members based at locations closer to their customers and target market could facilitate faster, cheaper and more efficient access to their local customers.

### 2. Improve Customer Intimacy

For sure, you can improve customer intimacy without being co-located with them. Technology has been a key enabler of improving customer intimacy remotely. Amazon and Google are great examples of this. They collect and assimilate all your activity on their websites, and turn this into intimate wisdom about you. Another example is an online fashion retailer which I consulted to. They have a strong brand and have built customer intimacy purely through virtual access to their customers. Through social media and online PR campaigns, they have increased customer engagement and have applied what they have learnt about their customers in gaining new customers.

However, for other organisations, getting physically close to your customers is an important route to customer intimacy. For example, having a trainer located in Germany, who is fluent in both English and German has helped me develop customer intimacy with my German-headquartered clients. Another example: one of my clients is a niche supplier of parts for refrigeration compressors. For four years they have struggled to win a tender with a prospective client in Texas. After establishing a local presence in Texas, they were not only awarded a contract with their much sought-after client within seven months of being there, but also gained further business from other local relationships in the US. Being physically closer to your customers means you have the opportunity to build better rapport by speaking their language, *literally and metaphorically*. You can adapt your sales and marketing strategies to local markets based on local cultures and buying behaviours. Some of this cannot be done remotely and is better achieved through a local presence.

## 3. Reduce Costs

Cost reduction is a common driver of strategic plans, and often a reason to establish distributed teams. Whilst the initial set-up costs may appear prohibitive, it is important to perform a review of total cost of ownership (TCO) against Total Expected Benefit (TEB). The strategic planning period will depend on the type of industry you are in. For example, I had a client in financial services that classifies themselves as a boutique investment bank. They were operating only out of the Isle of Man in the UK. They used my scorecard to provide a good platform for decision-making regarding whether they should establish a presence in other international territories. Their TCO and

TEB were calculated over a 5-year period. [Update at the time of writing this book: Based on low scores for the 5 drivers on my scorecard, they were unable to justify geographical expansion. Instead, they used some of the budget for growing their business through a network of international broker relationships and this seems to be effective.]

Examples of how TCO can be reduced in another country/territory include lower staff salaries, lower office leasing costs and lower utility costs. Apple still does its design projects in California, but has off-shored the assembly work to China. What about lower travel and accommodation costs? One of my clients is headquartered in Germany and is growing their business in Asia, particularly in Thailand and China. Two of their R&D Programme Managers amassed huge travel expenses as they were unable to communicate effectively with their customers in these territories remotely. After many failed Skype meetings and ultimately delays in product time to market, they found the only way to keep momentum on these projects would be to fly out and meet their customers face-to-face, often two weeks at a time several times a year. In the end, it was cheaper and more effective to lease a small office in Bangkok and have the two Programme Managers based there with a local support member of staff.

## 4. Access More Talent

Having offices in different locations means you have access to more talent. With technology as a key enabler for international collaboration, distributed organisations have the ability to use the best people for the job, regardless of their location. One of the organisations I had the privilege of working with is a global supply chain manager for its clients, specialising in procurement and logistics. Their "heads of" are based in different countries, e.g. Head of HR is in London whilst the Head of Sourcing is in Brazil, and the Head of Process & Knowledge is in the Netherlands. Their team members are based in different locations around the world. Being a Joint Venture organisation, their CEO is rotated every two years. When a job vacancy arises, their priority is to seek out the best talent, regardless of location.

## 5. Increase Productivity

Many organisations that established distributed teams have enjoyed an increase in productivity, and the ability to provide their customers a 24x7 service without having to pay staff over-time rates.

However, many teams experience a decline in productivity. "I sent them an email but have to wait for them to wake up to read it and by the time they reply I have already gone home. I'm waiting more than 24 hours for a response from my remote colleagues compared to my co-located colleagues." This is a common "complaint" and can be overcome with a bit more discipline in planning, time management and email management within the team.

A 2009 study by professors at MIT Sloan School and Harvard Business School revealed that distributed teams have out-performed co-located teams. They found the key ingredients to achieving increased productivity and reduce inefficiency are in task assignments and socio-emotional processes. In other words, distributed teams can enjoy an increase in productivity if most of their work is task-focused *and* there are frequent opportunities for relationship building within the team.

## How these Five Benefits Interrelate

If you consider the five benefits I briefly described, you will realise that they are interdependent. For example, improved customer intimacy should result in increased sales. Cost reduction could be driven by increased productivity and access to more talent.

If you are considering off-shoring or establishing distributed teams, use the scorecard below (or something similar) to assist in the decision process.

# 5 Benefits Evaluation Scorecard

I find when a group of executives have a scorecard like this to talk around, it is easier to be less emotionally attached to an idea and more objective in the decision process.

Distributed Team Benefit Evaluation Scorecard
version 1

| Potential Benefit | Likelihood Score 1-5 | Justification |
|---|---|---|
| Increase Sales | | |
| Improve Customer Intimacy | | |
| Reduce Costs | | |
| Access More Talent | | |
| Increase Productivity | | |

Likelihood Score

1 = no confidence at all that this benefit will be realized at all

2 = minor confidence that this benefit will be realized marginally

3 = some confidence that this benefit will be realized marginally

4 = extreme confidence that this benefit will be realized marginally

5 = extreme confidence that this benefit will be realized substantially

If you wish, you can insert a column to *weight* the potential benefits to have a weighted scoring. I am not keen on weighting for this scorecard, because for me this is not a detailed analytical assessment that pops out a number at the end and the number will say "go/no go". The scorecard is a tool to provide some structure to the discussion and evaluation of a go/no go decision. However, some executives find it useful to show relative importance of the potential benefits.

You may also want to add more rows to include other evaluation criteria. Other benefits some of my clients have used in their scorecards to aid in the decision-making process include risk reduction and operational efficiency.

## 7 Benefits Evaluation Scorecard - Weighted

Distributed Team Benefit Evaluation Scorecard version 2

| Potential Benefit | Likelihood Score 1-5 | Weighting Score 1-3 | Weighted Score | Justification |
|---|---|---|---|---|
| Increase Sales | | | | |
| Improve Customer Intimacy | | | | |
| Reduce Costs | | | | |
| Access More Talent | | | | |
| Increase Productivity | | | | |
| Risk Reduction | | | | |
| Improve Operational Efficiency | | | | |

Weighting Score

1 = important

2 = very important

3 = extremely important

**CHAPTER SUMMARY**

1. There are several benefits for establishing a distributed team structure, but with these come challenges too. However, we are operating in a global economy whether we like it or not, and there are few organisations that can afford to operate out of one location if their mission includes increasing turnover and profitability.

2. Use my Potential Benefit Evaluation Scorecard tool, or something similar, to appraise the benefits of your organisation establishing teams elsewhere against the cost of doing so. The scorecard can also be used to evaluate business initiatives that involve establishing teams elsewhere, like partnering with a 3rd party supplier.

3. The rest of this book assumes you are not in the decision process about whether or not to establish teams at remote sites, but are currently facing the challenges you have as a remote leader, so read on...

oooOooo

# 3| Assessing your Remote Leadership Complexity

*"What you cannot measure, you cannot manage."*

-Peter Drucker

**Tools and Templates in this Chapter:**

- Remote Leadership Complexity Assessment

The complexity of your remote leadership situation depends on a number of factors. It may be useful to have a benchmark of how complex your remote leadership situation is compared to others, and to know which factors are more signification than others. In this chapter, I share with you my Remote Leadership Complexity Assessment tool. The nine factors I have chosen for the tool do not form a complete list; these are the nine factors I believe are the most significant in assessing your remote leadership complexity. First, I'll explain each of the factors and how to score them. Then I invite you to complete the assessment and graph your results on a spider chart. Finally, once you understand the spirit of the tool, I encourage you to modify it and create your own with the factors that are relevant to your matrix and remote leading situation.

## Factors for Assessing Remote Leadership Complexity

### 1. Significant Relationships

For this first factor, think about the number of "Significant Relationships" you interact with at any one time.
Significant Relationships are:

- Any people that report directly to you if you are their line manager (regardless of their location) PLUS

- Any contractors that are reporting to you at least 60% of their time in your organisation, regardless of their location PLUS

- Your boss PLUS

- Any significant internal customer, client or supplier relationships *(significant means that you spend a lot of time communicating with them)*.

In traditional hierarchical organisation structures, it is much easier to work this out. Earlier versions of this assessment only had to consider the number of direct reports you have. However, most of my readers will find themselves in dynamic matrix organisation structures. If your situation is constantly changing, think of the number of Significant Relationships you interact with on *average at any one time.* Like all self-assessments, the score you provide should be one based on understanding the *spirit of the intent*, so you have a benchmark that reasonably reflects your current situation.

**Example 1:** Mike is a National Key Account Executive (UK) in the Construction industry. His job is to maintain strategic client relationships and build new relationships with prospective clients. He does not have a team under him, and therefore no line management responsibility. Any sales leads are passed on to the Sales team, any issues are passed on to the Operations team or to a Supplier where relevant. As he is field based, he has a home office, and his boss is based at the UK office in Crawley. Mike's number of Significant Relationships he has to interact with at any one time is dynamic. He has ascertained that at any one time, his Significant Relationships would comprise his boss, the Operations Manager and the key clients he is dealing with. Averaging out the number of client relationships he is managing, he has determined his number of Significant Relationships to be seven. Of course there are several other people he will interact with, including people in Finance, some suppliers and project managers. However, the amount of time he spends with these people is significantly less than those he has included in his number of Significant Relationships.

**Example 2:** Martina is a Project Manager and is working full time on a large project which is part of a larger programme. For the duration of the project, she is directly managing a contract Business Analyst who is co-located with her. The Programme Manager whom she indirectly reports to is based at a different location. Depending on the stage of the project, she is also managing about two other significant relationships that are not co-located with her (e.g. in the early stages, Legal and Procurement, in the later stages Head of IT and Senior Developer). Martina reports to her boss, the Project Sponsor, who is co-located with her. She has ascertained that her Significant Relationships at any one time is about five.

**Example 3**: Hans is Global VP Sales for a major credit card company. He has 18 direct reports around the world and his boss is based in a different location to him. His number of Significant Relationships is 19 – almost impossible to manage!

**Score 0** if your number of Significant Relationships is zero or one person.

**Score 1** if your number of Significant Relationships is two or three people.

**Score 2** if your number of Significant Relationships is four, five or six people.

**Score 3** if your number of Significant Relationships is seven, eight or nine people.

**Score 4** if your number of Significant Relationships is ten, eleven or twelve people.

**Score 5** if your number of Significant Relationships is greater than twelve people.

(feel free to use fractions in your scoring choice)

## 2. **Geographic Dispersion**

This relates to *how far* the various offices or working locations (for your Significant Relationships) are *from you, the remote leader.* The greater the geographic dispersion, the more complex your remote leadership situation. This dimension of complexity excludes time zone difference, which has its own score. You may be in the situation where you are managing, say, ten people all in the same time zone, but in different countries.

I have assumed that to be a remote leader you have to at least be leading someone that is not in the same office as you, i.e. not co-located. However, I once had a guy on my course who was managing an IT support team two floors below him. When I asked him why he was on the course, he said that he hardly sees them and most of his interaction with them is "remote". Fair enough!

For the purposes of this assessment however, the scoring is as follows:

**Score 0** if your Significant Relationships are all in the same office location, or all in the same city. This is whether you are all in one small office, a large building with several floors or an office campus.

**Score 1** if your Significant Relationships are in different locations in the same country territory but different towns/cities. For example *London and the South East* could be a territory in England; the *province of Andalucía* could be a territory in Spain, and *Quebec and Ontario* could be a territory in Canada. In the London and South East example, I could have four people in this territory based in Tower Hill (London), Brighton, Tunbridge and Redhill.

**Score 2** if your Significant Relationships are in different parts of the same country, i.e. if they are in *different territories or regions within the same country*.

**Score 3** if your Significant Relationships are in different countries in one economic region. Example Europe, Middle East, Africa, Asia, etc.

**Score 4** if your Significant Relationships are in *different countries in an international region*, e.g. Europe, Middle East and Africa (EMEA), Asia Pacific (APAC) or the Americas.

**Score 5** if your Significant Relationships are based across the globe in more than one of the above international regions. I hope you are not in this situation but I have met several professionals who are leading people in the Americas, EMEA *and* APAC. This is a very broad geographical span of leadership responsibility and can be extremely complex when it comes to team meetings and team management.

**Very Important Note**: The USA is an exception in the above scoring guideline. According to the above, if I have Significant Relationships in the states of Washington, California, Texas, Florida, North Carolina, Missouri, New York and Michigan I should score myself a 2 as they are all in the same country. This is not a fair comparison because of the geographical vastness of the USA. To be more accurate, I would score 3 in that example. If all my significant relationships are in the Midwest (e.g. Indiana, Iowa, Minnesota and Ohio) I would score a 2 rather than 1.

If you have teams across the Russian Federation or China, you can apply the same logic.

*Use the scoring as a guideline and if you're not sure, select a score that you believe more accurately reflects the complexity of your situation.*

### 3. Time Zone Difference

This factor takes into consideration the *maximum number of time zones you need to communicate across* to stay in touch with the people in your Significant Relationships.

For example, if you are based in London and have teams in South Africa, Germany, France and Sweden, your time zone difference is 1. If in addition to those countries you also have a supplier you interact with regularly in Kuala Lumpur, your time zone difference is 7.

Another example: If you are based in Paris and you are managing people in New Work, Toronto, Europe and Tokyo, your time zone difference is the maximum from Paris to the west (6) plus the maximum from Paris to the east (8) = 14 time zones.

**Score 0** if you work with your Significant Relationships in one time zone.

**Score 1** if you work with your Significant Relationships across two time zones.

**Score 2** if you work with your Significant Relationships across three to four time zones.

**Score 3** if you work with your Significant Relationships across five to six time zones.

**Score 4** if you work with your Significant Relationships across seven time zones.

**Score 5** if you work with your Significant Relationships across more than seven time zones.

## 4. Language Difference

This is the number of native languages in your Significant Relationships.

For example, if you are English and have two direct reports – one in Italy and one in Germany - and each of them are native Italian and German respectively, then the number of native languages in your Significant Relationships is three (including yours). However, you could have 6 managers, all in different parts of England, but two of them have different native languages (for example a Polish national and an Austrian national). In this case, the number of native languages in your Significant Relationships is also three. As a third example, you could have a native English speaker in your German office and a native English speaker in your Italian office that you manage. In this example, the number of native languages in your Significant Relationships is one, even though the three of you are each in different countries.

To keep it simple, you need not differentiate between different dialects of the same language. I live in Brighton, England, and quite often I have difficulty understanding the English spoken up north. Likewise, my Italian family in the north of Italy often battle to understand people in the rural south of Italy. This further level of complication is not considered in my model. Instead, I give you pause to smile.

Most international organisations have standardised on English as their international language. However, you will know that even though people can speak, read and write in English, the interpretation and understanding amongst people of different native languages can vary. This is often a key reason why communication is misunderstood. The greater the number of different native languages in your Significant Relationships, the more complex your remote leadership situation.

**Score 0** if there is only one native language represented in your Significant Relationships.

**Score 1** if there are two to three native languages represented in your Significant Relationships.

**Score 2** if there are four to five native languages represented in your Significant Relationships.

**Score 3** if there are six native languages represented in your Significant Relationships.

**Score 4** if there are seven native languages represented in your Significant Relationships.

**Score 5** if there are more than seven native languages represented in your Significant Relationships.

**Note**: The above scoring does not take into consideration the English language ability of the non-native English speakers. For example, people from The Netherlands have a very high standard of English. Once again, select a score according to the spirit of what we are trying to achieve with this assessment – the level of complexity you face for this factor.

## 5. **Cultural Difference**

This factor considers the number of *nationalities* in your Significant Relationships, which is different to the number of native languages. For example, you may have three significant relationships who are all native English speakers (one from the UK, one from Australia and one from the USA). According to the scoring for the previous factor, the Language Difference score is 0, but the Cultural Difference score is 3 (see below).

When scoring this factor, also consider where culture is vastly different within a large country, e.g. the USA, China and Russia. Use the scoring guideline below, and adapt it if necessary for the spirit of the assessment. As with my comment about language dialects, I am fully aware that even smaller countries like the UK have noticeable cultural differences between different regions. Focus on national cultures, and adjust your choice of score as you see fit.

**Score 0** if there is only one nationality represented in your Significant Relationships.

**Score 1** if there are two to three nationalities represented in your Significant Relationships.

**Score 2** if there are four to five nationalities represented in your Significant Relationships.

**Score 3** if there are six nationalities represented in your Significant Relationships.

**Score 4** if there are seven nationalities represented in your Significant Relationships.

**Score 5** if there are more than seven nationalities represented in your Significant Relationships.

## 6. Legal/Regulatory Difference

Different countries have different laws and regulations, which can make our remote leadership situation more or less complex. These include labour laws, tax laws, financial governance regulations and even business ethics regulations. The greater the number of country regulations affecting your work, the more complex your remote leadership situation when it comes to regulatory differences.

I initially tried to categorise this according to Economic Regions rather than countries, since Economic Regions (e.g. the European Economic Community) tend to have similar laws. However, I did not need to do too much research and investigation to discover that we still have vast differences in laws and regulations between countries within an economic region. Additionally, the "list" of world economic regions is continually changing, and this section would need to be re-written by the time I publish this book! So, at least for now, please base the score on the *number of countries* that, from a regulatory perspective, impact your work and those you lead.

**Score 0** for one country.

**Score 1** for two to three countries.

**Score 2** for four to five countries.

**Score 3** for six countries.

**Score 4** for seven countries.

**Score 5** for more than seven countries.

## 7. Effectiveness of Communications Technologies

Since most of your communication in the context of your role as a remote leader relies on technology, this is an important consideration. If the technology works and is fit for purpose, then that's great. However, so many times people tell me that their organisation has spent a fortune on implementing state-of-the-art video conferencing equipment that just doesn't work properly, so they revert to using telephone conferencing instead. Although it would be desirable, you don't have to have the latest bleeding edge tele presence systems. What's more important is that what you do have, *works as an effective communication enabler.*

For the purposes of this assessment, consider the technologies you have at your disposal for communication within your team/s, and how well these technologies enable efficient and effective communication.

**Score 0** if the communication technologies used are extremely good. The technologies used all work well, there are no problems in their operation and they are well-supported. There is no need for additional/new communication technologies.

**Score 1** if the communication technologies used are very good. The technologies generally work well, and there may be rare problems. There is no need for additional/new communication technologies.

**Score 2** if the communication technologies used are good. The technologies are generally effective in their use, but there is a need for additional/new communication technologies.

**Score 3** if the communication technologies used are poor. There are problems at least once a month that hinder communication.

**Score 4** if the communication technologies used are very poor. There are problems at least once a week that hinder communication.

**Score 5** if the communication technologies used are extremely poor. There are daily problems that hinder communication.

8. **Budget (Money and Time) for face-to-face meetings with your Significant Relationships**

Even though we are working remotely from our colleagues, having sufficient face-to-face meetings with team members is important. It often resets the glue in the team and provides opportunities for team problem solving and innovation in a manner that cannot be achieved through virtual sessions remotely. People often ask me "How much face-to-face time should I have with individuals and team members?" It really depends on the team in terms of the type of work they do, their level of competence, the quality of their relationships, and how much guidance they need. I would say you should see remote team members at least once a year. When we feel we do not have sufficient face-to-face meetings, the constraint is mostly either time or budget. In the scoring below, I have left it for you to be the judge based on whether you think the amount of face-to-face time you have with your team is satisfactory or not.

**Score 0** if you believe the amount of face-to-face time you have with members in your Significant Relationships is *completely satisfactory.*

**Score 1** if you believe the amount of face-to-face time you have with members in your Significant Relationships is *mostly satisfactory.*

**Score 2** if you believe the amount of face-to-face time you have with members in your Significant Relationships is *partially satisfactory.*

**Score 3** if you believe the amount of face-to-face time you have with members in your Significant Relationships is *partially unsatisfactory.*

**Score 4** if you believe the amount of face-to-face time you have with members in your Significant Relationships is *mostly unsatisfactory.*

**Score 5** if you believe the amount of face-to-face time you have with members in your Significant Relationships is *completely unsatisfactory.*

## 9. Experience in Remote Management

Finally, the more practical experience people have at remote leading, the better they get at it... often learning the hard way in the absence of training and coaching. Many times I have people attend my workshops who have been remote managers for over ten years, in highly complex environments. In my view, they have the QBE in remote management (Qualified by Experience) but they just don't know if they are doing it right, as they have never had training, coaching or even feedback from their colleagues. So they attend the course to see if what they are doing is "right". They leave the course with some additional insights, templates and tips that they wish they had 10 years ago, but they also leave with assurance that their experience has been a great teacher and coach, and some of the tips and tricks they have learnt along the way has served them well.

**Score 0** if you have had more than seven years' experience as a remote leader.

**Score 1** if you have five to seven years' experience as a remote leader.

**Score 2** if you have three to five years' experience as a remote leader.

**Score 3** if you have two to three years' experience as a remote leader.

**Score 4** if you have one to two years' experience as a remote leader.

**Score 5** if you have less than one year experience as a remote leader.

There may be other factors that affect the complexity of your situation, but these nine factors should give you a good measure of your remote leadership complexity.

I mentioned "Hans" earlier in this chapter. He was Global VP Sales for one of the world's largest credit card companies, and his Remote Management Complexity

Quotient was 82%. He had 19 Significant Relationships of which 18 were direct reports in different countries. He had employed a manager in Brazil nine months prior to me meeting him at the course. The job placement was based on what he thought was a good telephone interview with the candidate, and a successful local interview with the Office Manager in São Paulo. In the nine months that his Brazilian manager had been on board, they still did not have the opportunity to meet face-to-face. Guess where one of the problem regions was?

Initially Hans wasn't prepared to take my word for it – my word being that he seriously needed to reduce his Significant Relationships before he completely lost control (if fact, my opinion is that he had lost control). However, when he took part in the various exercises and discussions as the workshop progressed, he soon bought into the idea that he needed to territorialise his sales managers into three regions (the Americas, EMEA and APAC). He promoted three of his team members to lead the three regions, thereby reducing his Significant Relationships to just four (his three Regional Managers plus his boss located in a different country). We also worked out a plan for him to still stay in touch with everyone so that he didn't feel like he was losing control. I followed up with him 7 months later and he said it had made a huge difference – not only was he able to be more effective in his role, but his Regional Managers were being empowered and they were more effective in their roles too. This freed up his time to deliver more value at the strategic level rather than attempting the impossible job of managing 18 country managers and a boss across 14 time zones.

## Remote Leadership Complexity Assessment

(see next page for the template)

Once you have selected the most appropriate score for each of the ten factors, sum up your total score by totalling the right hand column.

You can then calculate your quotient and express it as a percentage as follows:

(Total Score/45) * 100

Example 1: If your Total Score is 24, your quotient is

$$(24/45)*100 = 53.3\%$$

Example 2: If your Total Score is 34.5, your quotient is

$$(34.5/45)*100 = 76.7\%$$

## Remote Leadership Complexity Assessment

| Assessment Factors | 0 | 1 | 2 | 3 | 4 | 5 | Score 0-5 |
|---|---|---|---|---|---|---|---|
| 1. Number of Significant Relationships (SRs) | 0-1 | 2-3 | 4-6 | 7-9 | 10-12 | Greater than 12 | |
| 2. Geographic Dispersion (of SRs) | Same city (e.g. London) | Same country territory (e.g. South East) | Same country (e.g. England) | Different countries in one economic region | Different countries in one int'l region | Different regions globally | |
| 3. Time Zone Differences (SRs) | One time zone | 2 time zones | 3 to 4 time zones | 5 to 6 time zones | 7 time zones | >7 time zones | |
| 4. Language Difference (Number of native languages in your SRs) | 1 | 2 to 3 | 4 – 5 | 6 | 7 | More than 7 | |
| 5. Cultural Difference - Number of different nations in your SRs | 1 | 2 to 3 | 4 – 5 | 6 | 7 | More than 7 | |
| 6. Regulatory Differences: Labour / Tax / other Laws/ Business Ethics | 1 country | 2 to 3 countries | 4 to 5 countries | 6 countries | 7 countries | More than 7 countries | |
| 7. Effectiveness of Communication Technology: fit-for-purpose quality | High quality communication systems | Good quality, minor issues | Average quality, some issues | Poor quality, several issues | Very Poor quality, significant issues | Completely ineffective technology | |
| 8. Budget (Time and Money) for F2F meetings with SRs | Completely Satisfactory | Mostly Satisfactory | Partially Satisfactory | Partly Unsatisfactory | Mostly Unsatisfactory | Completely Unsatisfactory | |
| 9. My Personal Experience in Remote Leadership | >7 years | 5 to 7 years | 3-5 years | 2-3 years | 1-2 years | <1 year | |
| TOTAL SCORE (sum) | | | | | | | |
| % Complexity (Sum total score out of max 45 points and convert to a %) | | | | | | | % |

You can also plot your scores for each of the nine factors on a spider chart to create a visual representation of your remote leadership complexity.

Example:

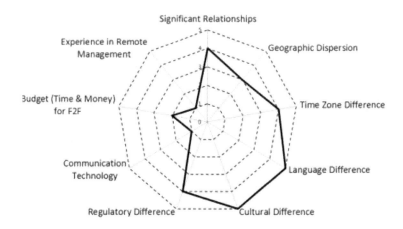

Score Interpretation:

< 20% = Non-complex remote leadership situation

20-39% = Fairly complex remote leadership situation

40-55% = Complex remote leadership situation

56-75% = Very Complex remote leadership situation

76-100% = Highly Complex remote leadership situation

## Relevance of the Complexity Assessment

As I mentioned at the start of this chapter, this assessment does not provide a comprehensive assessment of remote leadership complexity factors. Other factors that are less specific to remote leadership, i.e. factors that are equally present in co-located management, will also affect your remote leadership complexity. Such factors include (i) the capability and competence of individuals you lead; (ii)the job type that you are leading; and (iii)the industry you are working in.

Using this tool provides a benchmark of your remote leadership complexity across the nine factors. This might be interesting, but why is it useful ?

**Urgency** - The higher your Remote Leadership Complexity Quotient, the more complex your situation. The more complex your situation, the more rigorously and urgently you need to implement the best practices described in this book and perhaps work with your leadership team to make some improvements.

**Focus** – The factors that are the biggest contributors to your remote leadership complexity will be the ones you want to focus on. If you scored a 5 for each of Significant Relationships and Effectiveness of Communication Technologies, these are the areas you want to prioritise for focused improvement or better risk management.

**Benchmark for Strategic Planning** – It's good to have a benchmark of where you are now, and then anticipate what you think this might be in 6 months to a year from now. This is particularly important if your organisation (or your part of the organisation) is going through a growth phase. If you expect your team to grow, knowing in advance which factors can make your situation more complex will help you carefully think about your recruitment strategy, the organisation structure you design and the controls you implement to manage the risks associated with managing a geographically distributed team.

**Recruitment** – If you are going to be recruiting a remote leader, it will be helpful for you to think along these lines when writing up the job requirements, and for the candidate/s to understand the level of remote leadership complexity they may face.

## CHAPTER SUMMARY

1. There are a number of factors that can make your remote leadership situation more or less complex.

2. My Remote Leadership Complexity Assessment tool considers nine factors and provides a guideline scoring for your self-assessment.

3. When scoring, consider the spirit of the assessment and score yourself accordingly. For example, the guideline may say to score a '2' but actually you experience it to be a '3' in complexity. You can also allocate yourself fractional scores if that feels more accurate.

4. This tool is useful to help you make a case for improvement, to identify the factors to focus on, to use as a benchmark today when performing strategic planning for the period ahead, and for clarifying role complexity when recruiting for remote leadership positions.

oooOooo

## 4| Implementing a Code of Collaboration

*"Coming together is a beginning; keeping together is progress; working together is success."*

-Henry Ford

 **Tools and Templates in this Chapter:**

-Code of Collaboration Example

This chapter is relevant to you if you lead a team that has to collaborate remotely, for example international project teams, or functional teams such as a Regional Medical Science team or a global R&D team.

I begin by first refreshing on the Team Life Cycle according to Tuckman. You may well have seen this before in other books or training courses. However, I am including it here as I have met many team leaders that are not familiar with the Team Life Cycle. This model is important to lay the foundation for explaining the value of a Code of Collaboration for distributed teams.

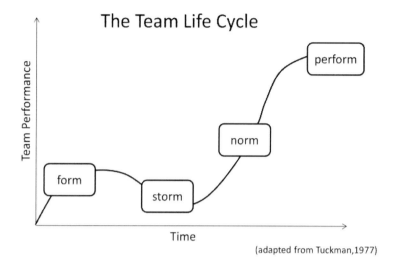

(adapted from Tuckman,1977)

A team is in the **Form** stage when:

1. it is a newly formed team, e.g. a project team or a new business unit;

2. the leadership of the team has changed;

3. the structure of the team has substantially changed;

4. the composition of the team has substantially changed; and/or

5. the working processes, roles and responsibilities of the team have substantially changed.

There is a level of performance in the team, and as they understand what needs to be done, performance starts to increase. However, it is very typical that one or more of the following could occur, which results in the team's performance decreasing. A team could enter into the **Storm** stage when:

1. there is resistance to change;

2. there is confusion or disagreement regarding roles and responsibilities;

3. the agreed working processes are not working or not being adhered to;

4. there is uncertainty regarding the future resulting in loss of morale; and/or

5. there are inter-personal conflicts between team members (overt or covert).

Once these problems are addressed, performance picks up and the team enters the *Norm* stage. It is called the Norm stage because at this point team members have a norm for how to collaborate.

A team would be in the **Norm** stage when:

1. changes have been deeply accepted;

2. roles & responsibilities are clarified and agreed;

3. working processes have been clarified, agreed and work as intended;

4. there is certainty regarding the future or tolerance for uncertainty; and/or

5. inter-personal conflicts have been resolved.

This dynamic is not particular to distributed teams; you will observe this in all sorts of teams. I am writing this chapter at the time when "The Island with Bear Grills 2016" has just concluded, and it was interesting watching the team pass through these stages. Watch any reality TV show that requires team members to work together, and you will see the same dynamic going from Form, to Storm, to Norm... and ultimately to the **Perform** stage.

When team members collaborate as a high performing team, you will evidence many of the following characteristics indicative of the **Perform** stage:

1. strong team identity

2. trust and respect within the team

3. effective communication

4. sense of empowerment and ownership

5. high task achievement

6. "can do" attitude

7. high level of enjoyment

Levels of performance in a team are never static as change is the constant, so we could have a number of further outcomes following the Perform stage, including the following:

1. The team could be disbanded, for example once a project is delivered. This is called the **Adjourn** stage.

2. Changes could occur which require the team to establish new or updated norms to quickly get back to the Perform stage.

3. Unchecked changes could be significant enough, causing the team to fall into the Form stage.

## The Team Life Cycle

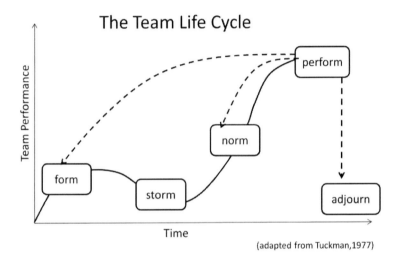

(adapted from Tuckman,1977)

## What is a Code of Collaboration ?

A Code of Collaboration is a set of rules — typically behaviours — that the team agrees to in order to collaborate effectively.

The astute Team Leader will facilitate the agreement of these rules with the team when they are in the Form stage, in order to pre-empt, or minimise the effects of, the Storm stage. In my experience, most often Team Leaders leave it until the Storm stage and then bring the team together to fix the problems, although by now some damage has been done. There is good reason in some cases to not facilitate the creation of a Code of Collaboration during the Form stage. This could be when:

- team members have performed well together previously;

- the team is not anticipated to enter the Storm stage (see examples of evidence in Storm stage above); and/or

- you are a new team leader and want to observe the dynamic in the team is first.

In most other situations, if your team is in the Form or Storm stage, it is a very good idea to bring them team together and discuss with them what they believe are the rules everyone should buy in to so that everyone can collaborate efficiently and effectively.

## What a Code of Collaboration is Not

It is not:

- your organisation's Code of Conduct

- a Code of Ethics

- standard operating procedures that have already been agreed in the organisation

*A Code of Collaboration is unique to the team, and relevant at that point of their evolution.*

**Example**: Below is an example from the Contracts Management Team of a mineral mining company. The team comprised eight managers located in different regions in Africa. Very often the contracts they were managing spanned overlapping regions, so they had to work closely together. I was leading a "Collaborating Remotely" training course for them, when it became clear that there were some very basic rules they had not agreed to, and these were causing them huge problems in working together and meeting deadlines. The Africa Contracts Management Team was well and truly in the Storm stage. Following our discussion on a Code of Collaboration, they decided to use the exercise time to develop their own.

These are the rules they agreed:

## Code of Collaboration Example

1. Monthly team meetings to be on the first Wednesday of the month at 3pm Johannesburg time.

2. Meeting Host and Note Taker to be rotated monthly in alphabetical order.

3. Meeting Host must sign in to WebEx with enough time to load all documents in advance of meeting start.

4. As a minimum, emails will be replied to within 24 hours of receipt, even if not with full answer. At least acknowledge receipt and when a full answer will be provided.

5. If a response to an email is not sufficient or understood, this must be followed up by a phone call, not another email. Schedule a call if necessary.

6. All scheduled phone calls and teleconferences to be treated as a professional meeting: preparation, punctuality and post-meeting actions taken.

7. All contract translations for China and Russia clients to be turned around within 2 weeks and stored in the appropriate folder on SharePoint.

Looking at these seven rules, you may ask yourself "But why weren't these obvious basics in place already ?" The reality is – and I have seen this time and time again – people are so focused on getting on with the job, they don't have the basics in place. With co-located teams it's easier to catch and address problems. But with distributed teams, it is important that the challenges of virtual collaboration are understood and proactively addressed by the team.

Not having the above agreements in place had two massive storming effects:

1. At an inter-personal level, there was conflict and distrust between team members.

2. At an operational level, the team's under-performance resulted in significant missed deadlines on the company's projects and tenders.

You can refer to your own experience to inform you that a lot of "micro-issues" cause macro-problems. Examples of micro-issues are people attending web meetings late, over-use of email when a telephone call would suffice, or surprising others with a missed deadline. Individually they may not seem like a big deal, but together these micro-issues result in macro problems.

In the above example, the value of the Code of Collaboration exercise was not so much in the document that was produced at the end of the session. Most of the value gained was in the discussion, understanding of the impacts of their behaviour and respectful agreements that were reached in that discussion.

## Topics Covered in a Code of Collaboration

There are a number of challenges that could benefit from a Code of Collaboration:

1. Virtual Communication - including meetings, email, instant messaging, telephone and texting behaviours.

2. Virtual Task Collaboration - including being accessible and do-not-disturb time.

3. Virtual Knowledge Management – how and where documents will be created, distributed, accessed and shared.

4. Virtual Problem Solving

5. Virtual Decision Making

In many cases, the problems new teams experience are largely to do with communication, so they call it a "Code of Communication".

## Criteria for a Code of Collaboration to be Effective

1. **Needs-based**.

Do not embark on this journey with your team unless you believe there is a need. Typically, there is a need when:

- You anticipate storming and you want to pre-empt or minimise the effects by having the team proactively agreeing how they should work together;
- Your team is in the storm phase and you want to push them out of it; and/or
- Your team is in the perform phase and you want to push them to collaborate even better together.

2. **TEAM Agreements, not the Team Leader's rules**.

In the next section of this chapter, I will explain how to facilitate the development of a Code of Collaboration. As the Team Leader, you are facilitating the process; the team members must come up with the agreements through your facilitation. When the topic of a Code of Collaboration was presented on one of my open courses, a manager put up his hand and said "I have tried this, and it did not work." I encouraged him to elaborate… He was promoted above his peers to take on the management of his team (they are procurement category specialists). Prior to his promotion, he was aware of a lot of problems in the team. He decided that one of the first things he would do is create a list of rules for the team to help them improve their performance. He wrote up what he called "Our Ten Commandments", emailed it to the team and advised it would be discussed at their next team teleconference. His intent was good, but execution was poor: 1.New Manager promoted above peers, i.e. already a level of resistance to his leadership; 2.He did not consult them and instead gave them his rules; 3.Not a good idea to call the rules Our Ten Commandments. I don't need to describe the scenario further for you to appreciate why it failed dismally.

3. **Development and implementation is a *process*,** not a one-off meeting.

This is what is *unlikely* to work: You get the team together at a conference venue and part of this off-site get-together you decide to facilitate the creation of a Code of Collaboration. It goes well, they come up with good stuff and all agree to stick to it. Three months later I call you and ask you how it went... you tell me that nothing much has changed.

This is what *is likely* to work: You email the team and ask them to each identify "one thing we could do as a team to collaborate more effectively". They are required to email you their idea in advance of the next team meeting (ideally a web meeting, not a teleconference). You consolidate the ideas and present it to them at the next web meeting. During the meeting, you facilitate the creation of a 5-8 point

Code of Collaboration based on their input. During the meeting, you ask each team member to give their thoughts on "how we can mitigate the risk of us not sticking to what has been agreed." Within 24 hours of the meeting, you distribute the Code of Collaboration, along with "How We Will Make it Stick". You tell them you will follow-up with them three months later to establish whether the rules resulted in improved team performance. You create a basic framework to assess before-and-after... etc. See my recommendations later, on how to facilitate a Code of Collaboration workshop.

4. **Should be documented**.

Even if you lead a mature team of professionals, the Code of Collaboration should be documented and not just left as a discussion. This will give it a degree of significance. Additionally, you may be leading an international team – some of them will benefit from having a written version of what was agreed. Finally, when you introduce a new member into the team, an explanation of the Code of Collaboration and how it is adhered to, is useful as part of their induction.

5. **Team members must have an appetite (buy-in or willingness) for this process**.

There may be a situation where you judge that this process will just not gain any buy-in from the team. This could be because you are their new team leader and need to prove yourself first, or their attitude is that this process is unnecessary and any problems in the team should be addressed on a case-by-case basis. Most often, teams welcome the opportunity to agree on how to collaborate well together through this process. However, I have worked with one team that flat-out refused. They were a team of Civil Engineering Project Managers reporting to a Programme Manager. The Programme Manager thought it would be good to have a Code of Collaboration agreed between the PMs for the Programme. They felt patronised and that there were more important things to focus on. The sentiment was "Collaborating together is a given, and we don't need to agree rules on how to do so." This movie does have a happy ending, as Programme dipped into the Storm phase early on, largely due to the "basics" not been agreed upfront. Different terminology was used (Programme Communication Protocol) but the essence of it was a Code of Collaboration which got them out of trouble.

6.  **Lead by Example.**

NEVER break the rules yourself.

Enough said.

## Guidance on Facilitating a CC Workshop

I have facilitated a number of workshops for team members to agree a Code of Collaboration. What I have found is that those that are facilitated virtually as part of a standard meeting (e.g. a monthly team meeting) are more effective than those that are agreed as part of a face-to-face team building or conference event. Why ? I believe that when people go to an off-site event, it is "off-site" – something that happens outside of our normal world of work. They talk about going "back into the real world" and there is less of an association with the rules that were agreed offsite.

If you are going to create a Code of Collaboration with your team, I would recommend facilitating it virtually, like the scenario I described above in the section "**Criteria for a Code of Collaboration to be Effective**". You can have the 3-month check-up as an agenda item at the face-to-face meeting. (It does not have to be three months you choose when is a good time to follow-up, typically between three and six months.)

In addition to my remarks in the section "Criteria for a Code of Collaboration to be Effective", below are some additional recommendations when facilitating the creation of a Code of Collaboration.

Forming to Norming

1. Present to the team the new situation (new organisation structure, new processes, your role, etc.)

2. Ask them to list the behaviours they all (and you) need to model in order to collaborate well together, particularly bearing in mind that some or all team members are working remotely from you and each other. They should focus on what is in their control, not things out of control (otherwise it becomes a dump of problems associated with the broader organisation).

3. Also ask them to list specifically the support they need from you.

4. For the items on the list that relate to their collaboration with each other, write these up as the team's Code of Collaboration.

5. For the other items, develop an Action Plan with them to ensure those factors are achieved.

6. Ensure tracking of the Action Plan with the team with sufficient frequency (weekly / every two weeks / monthly).

7. Three to six months later, have a discussion to evaluate effectiveness and agree "fine-tuning" agreements.

8. Throughout, keep a watchful eye on whether they are going to enter into a storming phase. This process should have pre-empted or minimised it, but please check.

If you are a Project Manager: A good time to do this is during the Core Team Kick-off Meeting (ensure you follow my guidance about this being a process, not just a one-off agenda item at a meeting).


Storming to Norming

1. Present the current scenario to the team. Show them the Team Life Cycle and ask them what stage they believe you are all in. They should agree the storm phase. If not, you have bigger problems! Assuming they agree you are in the Storm phase…

2. Get them to list the problem areas they are experiencing. You can then add any problems you have observed not on the list, but *first* get their contribution. Encourage them to focus on behaviours,

not personalities. Example NOT "The Brazilians always attend our Skype calls late." RATHER "Team members attending Skype calls late create a knock-on effect on..."

3. Ask them to filter the list so that you separate problems that are within the team's direct control and problems that are beyond their control.

4. For the problems in their control, facilitate a discussion on what they can do to resolve these issues and collaborate better together. Write these up as team agreements (aka a Code of Collaboration).

5. For the other problems, either turn them into an action for yourself, or put them into context for the team.

6. Follow-up as described in the section above "Criteria for a Code of Collaboration to be Effective".

**CHAPTER SUMMARY**

1. The spirit of a Code of Collaboration is to set the team's norms of behaviour so that they collaborate efficiently and effectively.

2. The aim of a Code of Collaboration is to create a team working culture that supersedes individual cultures, attitudes and behaviours.

3. It is especially useful for distributed team members, because the challenges associated with virtual collaboration often cause problems.

4. Most often, a Code of Collaboration is about getting the basics right; setting the foundation for the team to collaborate well together.

oooOooo

# 5| Nurturing Purposeful Remote Teams

*"Only the guy who isn't rowing has time to rock the boat."*

-Jean-Paul Sartre

 **Tools and Templates in this Chapter:**

-Remote Team Effectiveness Assessment

-RACI/PARIS Matrix

-1:1 DASH Meeting Framework

-Team Performance Dashboards

-Individual Task List for Matrix Managers

-Team Motivation Needs Assessment

## Understanding Purposeful Leadership

Several years ago I read an excellent article in the Harvard Business Review (Feb 2002 edition). It was titled "Beware the Busy Manager", by Heike Bruch and Sumantra Ghoshal. Their research revealed that for managers to be successful, they need to have high focus and high energy. Focus is what you need to be on target, and energy is the fuel that gives you the vigour to get a tough job done. A high-focus high-energy manager is what they called "purposeful", and you cannot have one without the other (focus without energy or energy without focus) to be purposeful.

In my subsequent research on effective remote teams, plus my clients' experiences of what works and doesn't work, I found the concept of "purposefulness" to be highly relevant to remote teams and their leadership. I have adapted Heike and Bruch's model by replacing "energy" with "engagement".

For remote teams to be effective, they need to be highly focused. Focus is not just about ensuring team members are given clear objectives to focus on. It is also about understanding what can *distract* their focus, and supporting them in a manner to keep them focused despite the distractions. An example of a distraction one of your remote team members may have, is having to prioritise work for a local office manager whilst still focusing on what you want them to do. Team members also need to be highly engaged. For me, energy is important, but *engagement* encompasses energy, enthusiasm, commitment and motivation. As a remote leader, my ideal remote team member is someone who can stay focused in an environment of never-ending distraction AND at the same time act with engagement.

The spirit of this Purposeful Model is about (i) *what* you do and (ii) the *way* you go about doing it.

If I have a team member that is highly focused but lacking in engagement, this will ultimately reduce their focus. Likewise, a team member that is highly engaged but lacking in focus, will ultimately become disengaged. We need to foster both to have purposeful teams.

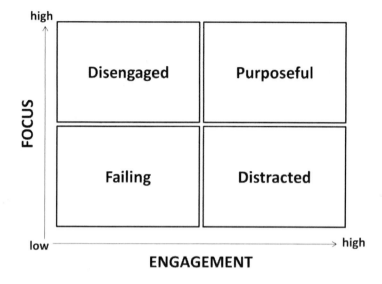

*Source: Adapted from Bruch & Ghoshal's Purposeful Leadership Model, 2002*

**Purposeful Leaders Keep Individuals and Teams FOCUSED by Giving Them:**

1. **Clear understanding of the organisation vision.** Team members are expected to *"think global, act local."* Ensure they understand the organisation vision in the context of their role, and give them training if necessary on how to reinforce the organisation vision through their work.

2. **Clear objectives** – This is a bit of a "no-brainer" but I have coached many remote team members to find that they were unclear on what was expected of them. As managers and team leaders, we sometimes forget that concepts we find simple to understand are difficult for others. Now bring in a good dose of misunderstanding due to language ability and cultural

differences. It then becomes understandable how objectives can easily become unclear. Some cultures or personalities will never ask for clarification, in fear that it may be career limiting. Because we work remotely from them, we discover too late that they lack focus because of unclear objectives. Objectives do not only need to be written, but clarified verbally for understanding. This brings me to my next point.

3. **Clear roles and responsibilities.** Team members need to be clear on the scope of their role, particularly if they are fulfilling multiple roles. For their role/s, they need to understand the responsibilities that go with that role. For some people, you need to ensure this is listed out in detail. For others, let them list it out and see if it meets your understanding and expectations.

4. **Contextual understanding of role**. Many people today operate in a matrix organisation structure. It is therefore essential that they do not only understand their objectives, roles and responsibilities, but also understand this in context of the broader organisation. They need to understand how their work impact's the work of other roles and vice-versa. It is important that you give them this bigger picture.

5. **Appropriate direction and support to achieve objectives**. I use the word "appropriate" because different people need different levels of support. The direction and support I refer to is not the feedback and direction you give at performance appraisals, or the scheduled 1:1 meeting you have with them. That goes without saying. I want you to think more operationally on a day-to-day basis. If you are co-located with a team member, it's easy to pass them and check in on them, or for them to ask for your help. *How are you*

*doing this remotely* ? You need to be virtually present when they need you. If you are working across one to two time zones, this can be a casual interaction of them calling you or instant messaging you when needed. However, if you are seven time zones apart, you need to be more structured to ensure you are present for them. Use technology to make yourself available to your team member seven time zones away for at least one hour a day. Try not to book meetings with people in Europe in the morning when your team member in Singapore is likely to need you. Another aspect of giving them appropriate support relates to the next point.

6. **Protection from distractions.** Managers and team leaders are pretty good at providing clear objectives, roles and responsibilities. However, where they often fall short is to recognise that their remote team members have to deal with a number of interactions that distract them from their focus. Examples of these distracting interactions could be local members of the organisation making requests of your team members because they have easy access to them, rumours about change in the organisation that could affect their morale, or having to work with ineffective technologies. Remote leaders should make it a priority to understand the types of distractions their team members face, and help protect them from these distractions by equipping them with the skills to better manage them.

7. **Information that keeps them afloat, not information that drowns.** Give them organisation updates and other information relevant to their jobs but do not overburden them with too much information. *Less is more.* If top management has issued a 20-page

organisation update, take it upon yourself to create a page of key points relevant to your team.

8. **Aligned Matrix Manager relationships.** One of the common complaints remote team members raise with me is that they have multiple reporting lines, and that the mangers they report to have different priorities, constantly changing priorities and regular disagreement on priorities. PLEASE get together with your peer group when you share resources in a matrix structure. Agree how you will share this resource and get the most out of them by keeping them focused and protecting them from unnecessary distractions.

9. **Authority matched with responsibility**. A team member is unable to successfully achieve the responsibilities that have been set for them without having the authority to do so, or support where their authority is lacking.

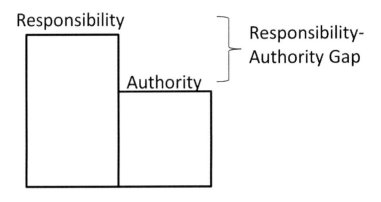

The reality is that authority will not always match responsibility. For example, a remote team member may be struggling in the responsibility-authority gap (RA Gap) when they lack:

- Signing authority to approve budget/spend.

- Decision making authority.

- Access to decision makers.

- Leadership authority.

- The ability to influence others they depend on.

Consider the people you lead. If they are operating in the RA Gap, consider whether you can i)reduce their responsibility, ii)increase their authority, or iii)trouble-shoot for them in the RA Gap. This is often when they will need your support.

This RA Gap dynamic is not unique to distributed teams, but it is more challenging for team members who have a job to do and most of their interaction is not face-to-face. Keep it on your radar and ensure you support them so that they can stay focused.

**Purposeful Leaders Keep Individuals and Teams ENGAGED by Giving Them:**

1. **FOCUS** - (all points above) PLUS:

2. **Recognition and appreciation** – People that work remotely from their managers often feel out of sight is out of mind. They feel over-worked, under-paid and under-appreciated as they have a sense that their efforts are not always visible. Find out what effort people are putting in to their work. If Tom in your team

has to travel a lot, and you know that this travel time infringes on his private time (not to mention that he works while he is commuting), recognise his efforts. I have more on this in the Motivation chapter later in this book.

3. **Sufficient autonomy and empowerment**. They keyword here is *sufficient*. Do not make the mistake of micro-managing highly competent people on your team.     However, people that are lacking in competence - or even confidence – may need more direction and less autonomy.  If you are not familiar with Situational Leadership as a concept, I recommend you brush up. This is basic management skills and essential for you to practice.   For team members to have the autonomy and empowerment they need to get on with the job, think about *"what do they need?"* Some will need software tools to make their job easier without always having to check with others; some will need direct access to decision makers; some will need more confidence coaching.   Empowering a team member is not a tick-box exercise of things you have handed over to them.   They may still not *feel* empowered.   Being empowered is a *feeling of empowerment*.   It will be different for different team members.  Find out what they need to feel empowered and act accordingly.

4. **The ability to make a personally meaningful contribution**. The key phrase here is *personally meaningful*. Similar to my comments about autonomy and empowerment, you need to know what *personally meaningful* means to each of your team members (this is particularly relevant to Line Managers).

5. **An inspirational leadership example**.  Even though you are remote from some of your team members, they are still watching you and learning from you.  Your virtual personality will be their blueprint for how to behave.  Encourage and value feedback on how you are perceived, and work on yourself as a leader that people want to follow.

**Sanity Check**: If you have someone in your team who is not sufficiently focused and/or engaged, remember this picture:

When you point your finger at them, only one finger is facing forwards; three are pointing right back at you whilst your thumb holds them firmly in place.  So before pointing at them about their lack of focus and/or engagement, ask yourself first what have you done or not done to help them.

It's not all about what you as managers and team leaders need to do.  There is also a responsibility on remote team members.  You want team members to take ownership of their focus and engagement, and let you know if they need your support.  Unfortunately, not all our team members have the attitude of ownership for various reasons.  These reasons could include culture/personality, previously been badly managed or just being overwhelmed with workload.  Encourage ownership. Explain what it means to take ownership by giving examples in the context of the work they do and the relationship dynamics they find themselves in.

Other than coaching and guiding current team member to be more purposeful as a remote worker, you have a *golden opportunity* when it comes to recruiting new team members. I am still shocked when I see job descriptions for professionals who will be operating in a virtual team or remotely from their manager, and the description does not cover specific attributes for the ideal remote team member. Neither does the interview. Read Chapter 14 "Recruiting the Ideal Remote Worker" for guidance on this.

**Useful Tools**

I am sharing with you some useful tools and templates that will help you stay on purpose with your team, and to help them stay focused and engaged. Not all tools will be relevant to you. Choose the ones you like and add them to your toolbox.

**Remote Team Effectiveness Assessment**

The spirit of this template is to assess your team's "health" against a set of key characteristics of high performance virtual/remote teams. Take a benchmark now, and measure it again in six month's time in the spirit of identifying opportunities for continuous improvement. My template has the following twelve characteristics against which to assess your team:

1. **Goal Alignment** – Team members at all locations have a clear and accurate understanding of the team's goals and objectives.

2. **Clear Roles and Responsibilities** – All team members are clear on their roles and responsibilities.

3. **Appropriate Empowerment** – Team members have an appropriate level of authority and empowerment commensurate with their job responsibilities.

4. **High Competence** – Team members are highly competent in their job function, requiring minimal leader direction on task achievement.

5. **Team Leader Virtually Available** – The leader of the team is sufficiently available when needed by individual team members and the team as a whole.

6. **Effective Communication** – Team members communicate using appropriate communication channels, with minimal delays, misunderstandings and misinterpretation.

7. **Decision Making** – The decision making processes in the team are effective and sufficiently efficient.

8. **Trust** – There is a high degree of trust between the remote team leader and remote team members, and between team members.

9. **Team Culture** – Team members have awareness and respect for each other's' cultures. The team has a high performance working culture, superseding individual cultures.

# Health Check: Remote Team Assessment

**Assessment**

0 = the team does not have this characteristic satisfied at all
1 = true for some of the team, *sometimes*
2 = true for some of the team, *most times* OR true for most of the team, *sometimes*
3 = true for all or most of the team, *most times*.

| High Performance Team Characteristics for Virtual Teams | Assessment | Comments/Actions |
|---|---|---|
| **Goal Alignment** – Team members at all locations have a clear and accurate understanding of the team's goals and objectives. | | |
| **Clear Roles and** Responsibilities – All team members are clear on their roles and responsibilities. | | |
| **Appropriate Empowerment** – Team members have an appropriate level of authority commensurate with their job responsibilities. | | |
| **High Competence** – Team members are highly competent in their job function, requiring minimal leader direction on task achievement. | | |
| **Team Leader Virtually Available** – The leader of the team is sufficiently available when needed by individual team members and the team as a whole. | | |
| **Effective Communication** – Team members communicate using appropriate communication channels, with minimal delays, misunderstandings and misinterpretation. | | |
| **Decision Making** – The decision making processes in the team are effective and sufficiently efficient. | | |
| **Trust** – There is a high degree of trust between the remote team leader and remote team members, and between team members. | | |
| **Team Culture** – Team members have awareness and respect for each others' cultures. The team has a high performance working culture, superseding individual cultures. | | |
| **Feedback down** – Team members receive accurate and timely feedback on company, team | | |
| **Feedback up** – Team members give accurate and timely feedback to their leader and peers on task status, issues and resolutions. | | |
| **Face-to-Face time** – The team takes time out with their team leader for evaluation, team building, celebration and performance improvement panning – at least annually. | | |

10. **Feedback down** – Team members receive accurate and timely feedback on company, team and individual performance.

11. **Feedback up** – Team members give accurate and timely feedback to their leader and peers on task status, issues and resolutions.

12. **Face-to-Face time** – The team takes time out with their team leader for evaluation, team building, celebration and performance improvement panning – at least annually.

**Remember**: *The model is not the model answer.* If you have attended my courses you may recall I say this a lot. Just because those are characteristics I have listed in the template does not mean that they are THE characteristics. By all means, use it as a starting point. I recommend you identify the characteristics that are relevant to *your* team and *their* remote/virtual working situation. Below are the frequently asked questions I get on my courses about this template, and my answers.

**Frequently Asked Questions About the Remote Team Effectiveness Assessment**

1. Q: *Can I use your template "as is" without modification?*

A: Of course you can, if you believe these would define the high performance characteristics relevant to your team.

2. Q: *If I wanted to develop my own Remote Team Effectiveness Assessment, how should I go about it and should I get my team involved?*

A: The more you involve your team, the better. You can have a face-to-face or virtual workshop with your team. Ask them to identify what they think would be the high performance characteristics of a distributed team such as themselves. Get them to select the top 10-12 characteristics and formulate a template from their input. Getting them involved and contributing to what they think are high performance characteristics gives you immediate insight into their level of maturity and understanding of what is expected from a high performing distributed team.

3. Q: *Who should do the assessment – me or my team members? If they complete the assessment, should it be confidential?*

A: It really depends on your team and how mature they are. For me, first prize would be for each person in my team to complete the assessment, and for their name to be known to me. This gives me immediate information regarding whether we are thinking the same. If their assessment is fairly similar to mine, then I can conclude that we are aligned and can work together towards continuous improvement. If all or some of their assessments are vastly different to mine, then I need to understand why, and this gives me an area to focus on. You can use tools like SurveyMonkey or just send out an Excel spreadsheet if you are unable to use a tool. If you meet with your team on WebEx, you can prepare a Poll in WebEx before the meeting and use the Poll feature for them take the survey live, share the results and as a team you can then discuss the assessment.

If you feel the team is in a Storming phase and there is some distrust in the team, then make it a confidential survey.

If you're going to have a face-to-face or virtual workshop to complete the assessment, do not have each person say what they think the score is in front of each other. In most cases, Group Think develops and you are not getting true individual responses.

I would also recommend that each person indicates a reason for their score choice in the "Comments" column – this is valuable information to you.

4. Q: *How often should such an assessment be completed ?*

A: It depends where your team is in the team life cycle. If you are in the Form or Storm phase, I would have them complete an assessment now, and immediately implement improvement actions. The follow-up assessment in this case should be three months later. If your team is in the Norm or Perform phase, I would say have a follow-up six months or a year later.

## RACI/PARIS Matrix

This is a popular matrix and many people are already using it. However, I am still surprised that when I show this on courses, at least one person in every group has never seen such a matrix. I am including it here as a useful template and will explain why.

. RACI is an acronym for:

1. **R**esponsible = those that will do the work.

2. **A**pprove = those that are accountable / will approve the output of that part of the process.

3. **C**onsult = those that need to be consulted by those that are responsible when doing the work.

4. **I**nform = those that need to be informed (by those that are responsible and/or accountable) that the work is taking place or once the work is complete.

You can create a RACI matrix for a project, such as in the example shown. You can also create a RACI matrix for any business processes that your team collaborates on, e.g. Supply Chain, Customer Support or Underwriting.

| Role | Location | Business Case | Project Charter | Detailed Specs | Design | Build | Test | Live | Evaluate |
|---|---|---|---|---|---|---|---|---|---|
| Project Sponsor | New York | R | A | - | - | - | I | A | A |
| Project Steering Committee | NY, London, Zurich, Singapore | A | I | - | - | - | I | C, I | C, I |
| Project Manager | Zurich | R | R | A | R | C, I | C, I | R | R |
| Head of Customer Services | Zurich | C | C, I | C | A, I | I | I | C, I | R, C, I |
| Customer Services Team Leader | Mumbai | I | C, I | R | C | I | R | R | C, I |
| Head of Product Development | London | C | C, I | C | A, I | I | I | C, I | R, C, I |
| Product Manager | Singapore | I | C, I | R | C | I | R | R | C, I |
| IT Development Manager | London | C | C, I | R | R | I | I | R | R, C, I |
| Business Analyst | London | I | C, I | R | R | C, I | R | R | C, I |
| Lead Developer | Zurich | C | C, I | C | R | R | R | R | C, I |
| Supplier | Hamburg | - | C | C | C | R | R | C | C |

R =Responsible (person that will do the work)   | A = Approve (person that is "accountable"/will approve the work)
C = person that needs to be Consulted   | I = person to be Informed about the work during or once it is complete

Variation – PARIS Matrix::  Participate | Approve | Responsible | Inform | Support

The first column on the left shows the role of the person. Here you can insert the role as in the example shown, and/or insert their name. I would insert role *and* name.

The second column shows where they are primarily based. This helps with communication planning and risk management.

The rest of the columns are for you to identify the key deliverables and/or key aspects of the business process where you would like to differentiate the roles and their responsibilities. In the example above for a project, we have Business Case, Project Charter, Detailed Specs, Design, Build (including system test), Test (user), Live and Evaluate.

Once you have created your template, you then need to insert how each role needs to engage with that process or deliver that deliverable

Traditionally, the A was for Accountable. The problem is, some languages do not have two words to differentiate Responsible and Accountable. When I work with international teams, I change the A to mean Approve.

In the example above, the Project Sponsor and Project Manager are responsible for producing the Business Case. The Head of Customer Services, Head of Product Development, IT Development Manager and Lead Developer need to be consulted in the production of the Business Case.

Once the Business Case has been drafted, it needs to be approved by the Steering Committee. Finally, once the Business Case has been finalised, the Customer Services Team Leader, Product Manager and Business Analyst need to be informed. There is a supplier in Hamburg that is not involved at this stage.

It can be quite a lot of work creating RACI matrices. However, this level of detailed analysis is very useful when there is confusion or disagreement about roles and responsibilities, or when the team is having to collaborate on a changed or new business process. In my experience, most people know who is responsible and accountable/approvers. Where things go wrong is when the right people are not consulted and informed (at all or at the right time). Having this matrix as a framework for assessments helps clarify how different roles need to be engaged in a business process.

Example

I was working with a restaurant chain in the UK to optimise their New Restaurant Opening Procedures. This restaurant chain was owned by a group company, which operated three restaurant chains. Each restaurant chain operated independently on operational matters, but shared business processes such as Supply Chain Management and Accounts Management.

Once I had identified the key steps in the restaurant opening procedures – from the time a new location was identified up to one month after opening – I asked my client to schedule a workshop to include the key players involved in the process. During the workshop, we agreed the key roles and locations for the two left hand columns of the RACI matrix, and then proceeded to agree for each part of the new restaurant opening process who should be responsible, accountable, consulted and informed. Within 15 minutes of the workshop, it became clear that one of the biggest problems that caused massive delays in restaurant openings is that Group Supply Chain representatives were not consulted early enough in the process. *It was so bad, that they were not even invited to our workshop!* This was a great learning for all concerned and subsequently a big time saver when we got them involved (consulted) earlier in the New Restaurant Opening Procedures.

You do not need a RACI Matrix if everyone in your team and relevant stakeholder groups are clear on roles and responsibilities. However, if clarity or alignment is lacking, then I believe you would benefit from agreeing one. The value is less in the final output, but more in the conversations that are held, and learning that is gained, when producing one. Also, if this is a key document for your team to clarify roles and responsibilities, don't make the mistake of emailing it to everyone expecting them to read and understand it. Ensure this is followed up with discussion to clarify contextual understanding. In some cases, training is necessary.

Variation

Once again, the model is not the model answer. You can choose the types of involvement based on the type of work your team does. For example, one of my clients does not use RACI but PARIS, where the acronym stands for Participate, Approve, Responsible, Involve and Support. The spirit of this template is to clarify how different roles, based in different locations, interact with a business process. I designed a responsibility matrix for a software company and called it DISCO (Do, Involve, Support, Consult, Own).

## 1:1 DASH Meeting Framework

The spirit of this template is to not fall into the trap (when you have your 1:1 meetings) of only discussing task status. Every scheduled meeting is an opportunity to keep people purposeful (focused and engaged). DASH is an acronym for Decisions, Actions, Status and *Happiness*.

**Decisions**: What decisions have *they* made that you need to know about since you last met? What decisions have *you* made that they need to know about since you last met ?

Actions: What actions are agreed as a result of this meeting and when will they be completed?

Status: What is your and their status with regards to tasks and actions previously agreed?

Happiness: How are they getting on at the local operation ? Do they need anything from you ? How can you better support them? If you are their line manager: Have they identified career development opportunities?

Clearly, the above does not reflect the order of the Agenda, so I have included a template below where the order is Status, Decisions, Happiness and Actions.

---

## 1:1 DASH Meeting

Date, Time & Channel: _____

Meeting with:_____        Their Location: _____
Last 1:1 Date: _____        Channel: _____

Status:

Decisions:

Happiness:

Actions:

---

Create your own if you don't like mine, but please remember that your 1:1 meetings should not just be about focus (i.e. task status); they should also about nurturing engagement.

## Team Performance Dashboards

In addition to your DASH meeting notes, it is useful to have a dashboard showing each team member's performance in summary form. I have two examples to share with you. One is for a team of Business Development Managers, the other for a Team of Project Managers. This book is printed in black and white. You should use red, amber and green on the dashboard to show a visual representation of performance.

## Monthly Team Performance Dashboard: Business Development Managers

Date: 30 October 2015

| Team Member | Location | Last 1:1 | Next 1:1 | Target Achievement | Task Achievement | Relative Productivity | CCQ | Customer Feedback | Overall | Action |
|---|---|---|---|---|---|---|---|---|---|---|
| Anton | Lyon | F2F in London 2 Oct 2015 | Tel Meeting 14 Nov 2015 | □ | → | → | → | □ | → | |
| Baz | Kuala Lumpur | WebEx Meeting 5 Oct 2015 | WebEx Meeting 15 Nov 2015 | → | □ | □ | → | → | → | |
| Lutz | Hamburg | Tel Meeting 20 Sep 2015 | Tel Meeting 14 Nov 2015 | □ | ← | □ | → | □ | → | |
| Jose | Madrid | Tel Meeting 6 Oct 2015 | Tel Meeting 14 Nov 2015 | ← | ← | → | ← | □ | ← | |
| Michael | London | F2F in London 25 Oct 2015 | F2F in London 6 Nov 2015 | □ | □ | □ | □ | □ | □ | |
| Sarah | Leeds | F2F in London 2 Oct 2015 | Tel Meeting 14 Nov 2015 | □ | □ | □ | ← | ← | □ | |
| Stefania | Tunn | Tel Meeting 6 Oct 2015 | Tel Meeting 21 Nov 2015 | □ | □ | □ | → | □ | □ | |

**Performance**

☺ Excellent, no problems
☺ Good, self-managing problems
☺ Average, needs guidance to improve
☺ Below-Average, needs local on-the-job coaching
☺ Poor, investigate urgently
☺ Unacceptable, marginal

**Trend**

↑ improving
□ same
→ worse

**Abbreviations**

CCQ = Customer Contact Quotient

Example 1: Team of Business Development Managers

1.  Insert the name of each team member in the first column.

2.  Insert where each team member is based in the second column.

3.  In the third column, indicate when was your last 1:1 with them and via which channel of communication.

4.  In the fourth column, indicate when is your next scheduled 1:1 with them and via which channel of communication.

Typically, your template should have the above first four columns regardless of job type. The rest of the columns are specific to their job. For the team of Business Development Managers, I have chosen to assess them monthly in six areas:

- Target Achievement = meeting their business development targets.

- Task Achievement = getting other things done, such as commercial reporting.

- Relative Productivity = how productive they are given my understanding of how much time they spend getting things done.

- CCQ = Customer Contact Quotient, a Key Performance Indicator (KPI) of how many new customers they are engaging per month.

- Customer Feedback = my assessment based on monthly feedback I get from current customers about their relationship with the Business Development Manager.

- Overall = an overall assessment about how I feel the team member is doing.

In each block for each team member, I am showing my assessment of how they are doing and a trend to show better, worse or the same.

Finally, the last column is for notes to remind yourself of why you have assessed the person in that way.

Example 2: Team of Project Managers

For the Project Managers, I have the same first four columns. The Key Performance areas I am assessing for them are:

1. Time Management = meeting deadlines.

2. Stakeholder Management = how well they are managing the project stakeholders.

3. Team Management = how well they are leading their core team.

4. Overall PM = their overall project management ability.

In this template, I not only have a Comment column, but also an Action column. The Action column is for the actions I need to take to support their performance.

## Monthly Team Performance Dashboard: Project Managers

Date: 30 October 2014

| Team Member | Location | Last 1:1 | Next 1:1 | Time Management | Stakeholder Management | Team Management | Overall PM | Comment | Actions |
|---|---|---|---|---|---|---|---|---|---|
| Anton | Lyon | F2F in London 2 Oct 2014 | Tel Meeting 14 Nov 2014 | | | | | | |
| Baz | Kuala Lumpur | WebEx Meeting 5 Oct 2014 | WebEx Meeting 15 Nov 2014 | | | | | | |
| John | Munich | Tel Meeting 20 Sep 2014 | Tel Meeting 14 Nov 2014 | | | | | | |
| Jose | Madrid | Tel Meeting 6 Oct 2014 | Tel Meeting 14 Nov 2014 | | | | | | |
| Michael | London | F2F in London 25 Oct 2014 | F2F in London 6 Nov 2014 | | | | | | |
| Sarah | Leeds | F2F in London 2 Oct 2014 | Tel Meeting 14 Nov 2014 | | | | | | |
| Stefania | Turin | Tel Meeting 6 Oct 2014 | Tel Meeting 21 Nov 2014 | | | | | | |

Actions Applicable to all:

**Performance**
- Excellent, no problems
- Good, self-managing problems
- Average, needs guidance to improve
- Below-Average, needs focused coaching
- Poor, investigate urgently
- Unacceptable, marginal

**Trend**
- ↑ improving
- □ same
- → worse

**Definitions**
- Time Management: Ability to drive planning by critical path
- Quality Management: management of KPI's (e.g. ppm, TTM)
- Team Management: Ability to distribute tasks and to get best of core team members
- Overall PM: general performance based on Time, Quality & team Management, plus + general behaviour

*Remember*, the model is not the model answer. These are just two examples of team performance dashboards. The spirit of the dashboard is to have a monthly view of the team's performance as holistically as possible. By holistic, I mean not just typical KPIs like meeting sales targets, but other aspects that reflect on focus and engagement. This is information or insights you should have already. Completing a line for each person should not take more than 10 minutes. If I have seven people in my team, it should take me about 1½ hours to complete the dashboard each month. This is time well spent as I am stepping back from the detail and assessing how team members are doing. I am not conducting a full-blown performance appraisal. This is a monthly assessment of how focused and engaged they are. This consolidation will help me decide whether the team as a whole is struggling, or which individuals I need to get closer to – virtually or face-to-face if required. The trends tell me if the actions I/we are taking are working. This is also a useful tool as input to an annual or bi-annual performance appraisal. Reflecting on someone's performance over the last six months is not that easy. We tend to recall more recent events. This shows performance benchmarks monthly over time.

The tool is useful not only for line managers. I was coaching a Programme Management Office (PMO) Head. The Programme Managers did not report to him directly – they all had their own line managers for the technical platforms they were specialised in. The PMO Head was tasked with improving programme delivery, which required behaviour change from these specialists. The Programme Manager Team Performance Dashboard was an invaluable tool for him to track monthly behaviours of each of the individuals, and provide purposeful coaching to them.

People often ask me if the Team Performance Dashboard should be shared with the team. My answer is NO, this is your tool. You can share each line with the relevant team member. In fact, I encourage you to get team members to self-assess. It is really useful to understand if their perception of their performance is the same as yours. If you have a weekly 1:1 DASH meeting, each month you can add 15 minutes to the meeting and include the performance assessment.

As a remote team leader, this is an essential tool to keep your finger on the pulse of things. In a co-located situation, it is much easier to have a good idea of how people are doing. But with team members distributed across different locations, this is a great way to facilitate your thinking in a structured way about how each person is doing, and for them to do the same of themselves.

## Individual Task List for Matrix Managers

This is not a template for you to complete, but one you may recommend a team member to complete. If you have a team member operating in a matrix organisation where they are delivering work for you and one or more other managers, it is useful for them to visualise their workload for each of their managers in this way. They should also send it to each of their managers so that you can all see how you can help the matrix team member focus and prioritise better.

In this example, Tom Jones is a Senior Underwriting Analyst and works from home in Brighton if he is not required at the London office. He reports to Miguel Gonzalez in Madrid and to John Walker in London. He has a set of tasks/deliverables that need to be performed for each manager. These are shown in the middle column, along with the deadline in the next column. Tom has estimated how much effort is required to complete each task, and is showing a red/amber/green assessment regarding whether the task is likely to be completed on time. Red and amber assessments are accompanied by Explanatory Notes, which can be inserted in a column to the right or in a separate section below the table.

Task List for My Matrix Managers

Name: Tom Jones    Job Title : Senior Underwriting Analyst
Office Location: Brighton (I work from home and comes into London office as required)
Last updated: 25th May 2017

| Manager \| Location | Key Tasks | Deadline | Estimated Effort Remaining | RAG Status & notes |
|---|---|---|---|---|
| Miguel Gonzalez | 1 | 2 Jun '17 | 14 hours | i |
| | 2 | 10 Jun '17 | 27 hours | ii |
| | 3 | 31 May '17 | 6 hours | |
| Madrid | 4 | 16 Jun '17 | 4 hours | |
| John Walker | 1 | 9 Jun '17 | 18 hours | iii |
| | 2 | 27 May '17 | 5 hours | iv |
| London | 3 | 26 May '17 | 12 hours | |
| | 4 | 11 June '17 | 2 hours | |
| | 5 | 11 July '17 | 2 hours | |
| | 6 | 22 Jun '17 | 8 hours | v |

Explanatory Notes:
i.
ii.
iii.
iv.
v.

As I mentioned previously, this is not a template that you would complete. This is something you would recommend Tom updates monthly and shares with you and his other manager/s. The benefit is largely for Tom, as you want him to take ownership for visualising his workload for multiple managers, to prioritise what needs to be done and to ask for help when needed. However, the benefit is also for you and the other managers as you can see how much Tom has going on at the moment, and whether he has capacity for more. If he is struggling, this is an opportunity for you and the other managers to negotiate priorities and get Tom back on track.

Create your own template if you don't like this one, or get "Tom" to create his own. The spirit if this template is to have the workload of matrix team members visible and transparent to all relevant managers.

**Very Important Note**: This template is useful if your organisation has not invested in tools which show team activity. I have included it because many of my clients still default to MS Word and Excel to document team activity. However, there are a host of software tools which show team activity. Have a look at the Appendix "Project Workflow and Collaboration Tools" where I have listed popular software tools that some of my clients use.

Tools like Slack, Jira, Trello and KanbanFlow are a great replacement for a template like the above Task List. Use a software tool with your teams if you can. Alternatively, use a template like the one I share here to ensure that Matrix Workers keep their workload visible with their matrix managers.

## Team Motivation Needs

Earlier, I said that engagement encompasses energy, enthusiasm, commitment and *motivation*.

Motivation is largely about needs satisfaction. If you want to motivate your remote team members, you need to understand what they need. The template below is to facilitate your thinking about each team member and the team as a whole.

Team Motivation Needs Assessment

| Team Member | What they Individually Need from Me Currently | What they ALL need from me Generally |
|---|---|---|
| Lütz (Hamburg) | | |
| Eva (Amsterdam) | | |
| Erik (Berlin) | | |
| Janis (London) | | |
| Jeanne (Paris) | | |
| Björn (Oslo) | | |
| Tomislav (Zagreb) | | |
| Sergei (Moscow) | | |

For each team member, write down what they currently need from you. Some people may need you to spend more time with them, others may need you to back off and let them get on with the job. Some team members may need more recognition for their efforts, and others may need their work to be more visible to their colleagues. It is also worth reflecting on what the team as a whole needs. If they are in the storm stage, they may need unity and clarity. If they are in the perform stage, they may need an opportunity to have some fun team building.

I have included this Motivation Needs Assessment template here as it is relevant to this section on nurturing purposeful teams. I reflect in more detail about motivating remote teams in the next chapter.

**Team Code of Collaboration.**

Already discussed in Chapter 4. This is a great tool to keep teams focused on what is expected in terms of how they should collaborate and to increase engagement with each other.

## Evaluating Purposeful Status with your Team

**TIP:** Next time you have a face-to-face meeting with your team, explain the Purposeful Model to them. Then divide them into two groups and ask them to write up the following flipcharts: Group A should discuss and write up "Factors Negatively Impacting our Focus"; Group B should discuss and write up "Factors Negatively Impacting our Engagement".

Once you have a list, you should sort it (with them) into one of three categories:

1. WE Should Address, e.g. "email distractions"
2. Our Team Leader Should Address, e.g. "lack of visibility of our work with senior management"
3. Organisational Reality, e.g. "too much change"

You are likely to see some overlaps between the two lists, as sustained problems with engagement will affect focus and vice versa. This exercise will give you excellent wisdom about your team's first-hand experience and an opportunity to not only support them better but help them take ownership of these challenges and operate more independently.

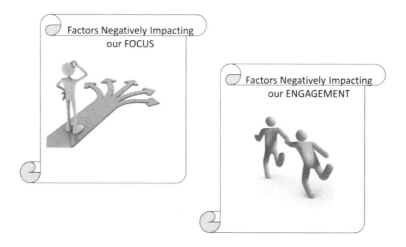

**Note**: I have recommended that you facilitate this exercise with your team during a face-to-face session. Of course, you can facilitate this virtually with them too. I have found this exercise to be more effective when performed in a co-located environment as team members are away from their local offices and think more objectively about it. This is different to creating a team Code of Collaboration where sustainable results are best achieved on-the-job.

## CHAPTER SUMMARY

1. Remote leaders should aim to keep their teams purposeful, which is a function of high focus and high engagement.

2. You can't see your remote team members, so don't stress about how much time they spend in the office. Shift your focus to measuring outputs, not inputs.

3. Focus encompasses having clear objectives and expectations to focus on, and managing the environment of distractors that could negatively impact focus. Engagement encompasses energy, enthusiasm, commitment and motivation.

4. I have listed important points you should check off to ensure you have supported your team's focus and engagement.

5. I have shared with you some useful templates that will help you stay on purpose with your team, and to help them stay focused and engaged. Not all tools will be relevant to you. Choose the ones you like, combine them and modify them to make them relevant to your world of work.

6. A Code of Collaboration may also help your team be more focused and engaged.

7. I recommend you share the Purposeful Model with your team, and at the next opportunity have a workshop with them to understand and address negative impacts on their focus and engagement.


oooOooo

# 6| Motivating Remote Team Members

*"Leaders become great not because of their power, but because of their ability to empower others."*

-John Maxwell

This chapter will be brief as I do not want to regurgitate popular motivational theories that are not specific to the remote working situation. If you are not familiar with popular motivational theories, I suggest you look up Maslow and Herzberg for a start. There are many other theories, and most of them boil down to *needs satisfaction*. In essence, individuals are motivated to take action when that action satisfies, or is perceived to satisfy, one or more of their needs (example needing more money, needing to be stretched intellectually, needing recognition, etc.).

### 7 Common De-Motivators for Remote Team Members

When I interview remote team members about what de-motivates them most, these are typically de-motivators they raise:

1. My work is not visible to my manager.

2. My work is not appreciated.

3. I am overloaded and they can't see it.

4. It's confusing reporting to multiple people.

5. I don't experience the social aspects of co-located teams.

6. It's lonely working at a remote office on my own.

7. I have to travel too much.


## 7 Key Considerations for Remote Motivation

1. **Understand de-motivators specific to virtual/remote teams**. This is always a good place to start. In a previous chapter, I recommended you meet with your team to discuss "Factors that Negatively Impact Engagement" – these would typically be their de-motivators.


2. **Understand individual personal motivational drivers**. Each person is driven uniquely. If you apply the spirit of my 1:1 DASH meeting and the Motivation Needs Assessment, you can find out what motivates individuals in your team. For some it may be about career advancement, others it may be about more autonomy, whilst others it may be about having more access to you. Find out what individuals need from you and act accordingly.


3. **Choose an appropriate Channel of communication when giving recognition**. Assuming you are remote from your team members, think about the best way to give recognition. Should it be in an email to them ? A telephone call ? A web meeting with the whole team ? Some people would prefer you to write an email which

they can read, understand and show their family. Others would prefer a team announcement, whilst others would prefer a mention during your next 1:1.

4. **Observe the Law of Diminishing Returns**. This is something I learnt in Economics 101 and equally applies to how recognition is valued. Example: Imagine Jane is a new member of the team and has recently done some excellent work. You send her an email to thank her for a job well done. This is the first time she has received recognition from her boss. The value of this recognition on a scale of 1 to 10 is 10. She beams all day with delight and tells her husband when she gets home. She is now even more eager to please and continues to exceed your expectations. You send her another email, similar to the previous one. However, she is expecting this, so the value is now 8 out of 10... and so on until eventually she is sanitised to your style of email recognition and the value goes right down. Read the section after this "21 Tips to Motivate Remote Team Members" to get ideas about how to show recognition in sincere and unexpected ways. Be creative, not because you *should* but because you *care*.

5. **Encourage self-understanding and self-motivation.** The first four points in this section are about what *you* should do. However, it is important to encourage team members to take ownership of *their* motivation. Motivation is largely a state of mind, and the best person to manage that state of mind is the person owning it. Have open discussions with team members

about the challenges and benefits of remote working. Encourage them to self-assess and develop self-motivation strategies that work for them.

6. **Consider Personality Profiling.** This is a great way for individuals to better understand themselves and for you to understand them. Popular profiling tools at the time of writing this book are Myers-Briggs, DiSC and Insights. There are many more and you can even find free tests on the internet. I have also developed a profiling tool called PersonaPro™ which I use to front coaching engagements or as part of relevant training courses - get in touch if you want to know more about it. Whichever tool you use, Personality Profiling is a great way to get to know the personalities of those you lead.

7. **Cultural expectations and values.** Culturally, some people prefer receiving recognition in front of others whilst others may prefer this in a 1:1 discussion. Read the excellent works of Hofstede and Trompenaars to understand how culture affects people's expectations of how they should be managed and motivated.

## 21 Tips to Motivate Remote Team Members

In this section I share with you some tips that I have picked up along the way. Not all are relevant to each member of your team or for the type of team you lead. The spirit of this is *"think creatively and really care."* I have grouped these tips under the headings of Abraham Maslow's higher-level needs from Social, to Self Esteem to Self-Actualisation.

### Social Needs (the need to have identity with a group/s)

1. Have at least one co-located team-building event per year.

2. Encourage team members to use instant messaging technologies and related apps if this does not interfere with their work (it often speeds up work !). Instant messaging is the closest we can get to virtual "water cooler discussions." Use instant messaging to check in with team members – not only about work but about how they are doing or just to say hello.

3. Don't feel threatened when remote team members form strong relationships with local teams at the remote site. Instead, when reminding them of your priorities and objectives, also show an interest and ask them about the local culture and camaraderie they have with co-located persons there.

4. Send occasional eCards for important "social" milestones (birthdays, marriage, etc.).

5. Create an intranet site or electronic bulletin board for your team. Display information updates, team organisation chart with photos, roles and responsibilities, Q&A, etc.

6.  Allow team members to access their social networks, provided this does not interfere with their work or cause information security breaches.

7.  If possible, and for those that are interested, organise a location site visit programme. Let team members visit colleagues at other offices to see how things are done there.

## Self Esteem Needs (the need to feel appreciated and respected)

8.  Write your remote team member a personal note of congratulations for excellent performance on handling a difficult situation.

9.  Send an appreciation email and cc your manager/other team members.

10. Get your manager to send an appreciation/recognition email to someone in your team, if that person is used to receiving recognition from you.

11. For team members that have to travel a lot, give them some "unofficial" time off when they get back or as soon as work allows (morning off, afternoon off, up to a day off).

12. Ask *your manager* to attend a virtual meeting with your team during which you recognise their achievements.

13. Send an appreciation letter to a team member's family, thanking family members for their understanding and support when this person had to put in long hours away from home.

**Self-Actualisation Needs (the need to realise all of one's potentialities)**

14. Help them see the purpose and value of their contribution in the context of the broader organisation mission and vision.

15. Give them the relevant autonomy matched with their capability to do a great job.

16. Help them see progress in their career development – progress motivates!

17. Ask team members for their ideas on problem solving, optimising team effort, etc. If you do this, be prepared to act on these ideas.

18. At your team meetings, share information from other meetings you attend within the company, industry journals you read, etc.

19. Give them more responsibility when they ask for it.

20. ASK them what their career aspirations are and whether they feel their full potential is being used. Discuss how you can support them in their career development.

21. Give them the opportunity to explore other opportunities in the organisation if this is of interest to them.

**Very Important Note:** I encourage you to also think about what motivates and de-motivates YOU. Develop your self-motivation strategies. Ask yourself whether you ACT as a motivational leader when you interact with team members. Do you use positive and confident language, whether in email or dialogue? If you are de-motivated yourself, this will transfer to your team members.

Your priorities are:

1. **Be** motivated.
2. **Act** motivated.
3. **Take specific actions** to motivate individuals in your team.

**CHAPTER SUMMARY**

1. Motivation is about needs satisfaction. Understand what individuals in your team need, and play a role in supporting them accordingly.

2. Bear in mind the seven key considerations when deciding how to motivate remote team members.

3. Be creative when motivating remote team members. Think about their social needs, self-esteem needs and self-actualisation needs.

4. Refresh your knowledge on popular motivational theories if you have not done so already.

5. Ensure you stay motivated as your state will transfer to others.

oooOooo

# 7| Working Effectively with Different Cultures

*"Studying culture without culture shock is like practicing swimming without experiencing the water."*

-Geert Hofstede

There are a huge number of books available on culture, and some people have made understanding culture their life's work. However, this book would be lacking if it did not include my recommendations on working with different cultures. In this chapter I am going to share with you three things:

1. Ten Key Considerations for Working with Different Cultures

2. Two Books on Culture I Have Read and Recommend

3. Two Websites on Culture I Have Used and Recommend

## 10  Key Considerations for Working across Cultures

### Be Respectful

1. Show respect and sincere interest in other cultures.
2. Research is good; local knowledge is best.
3. Update your calendar with religious and public holidays of your team members, and check before scheduling meetings.

**Be Specific**

4. Clarify your expectations regarding dates and times for task deadlines, as specifically as possible.

5. Check understanding using open contextual questions (see below).

**Be Flexible**

6. Change your approach to get the most out of your interaction with people of different personality styles.

7. Your natural management style may not be the best approach for the culture/personality you are managing.

8. Don't take it personally if you have been culturally offended. It was not intended.

**Be Professional**

9. Focus on what the team agrees on, not on its differences. Example: the team agrees to be punctual for all meetings

10. The team working culture should supersede individual cultures without negatively impacting on individual values. (A Code of Collaboration can facilitate this)

## Examples of Open Contextual Questions

You may have had the experience that some cultures or personality types will say they understand an instruction when in fact they do not. When you are delegating work, it is important that the team member understands what they need to do and what is expected. On courses, I ask "How do you know if someone has understood your instruction?" The most common response is "I ask them to tell me what they have understood my instruction to be." This is not necessarily clarifying their understanding. It merely clarifies that they were listening and can reflect back to you what you have said. By all means, do this. Then follow up with open contextual questions. These are open questions to clarify their true understanding of what you are delegating and their ability to deliver. Below are examples of open contextual questions:

"How will you fit this in with your other priorities ?"

"Who do you think are the key decision makers in this process ?"

"What do you think are the key risks associated with this task?"

"Which other offices would need to be consulted in the process?"

## Two Excellent Books on Culture I Recommend

1. *Kiss, Bow or Shake Hands*, by Terri Morrison and Wayne A. Conaway

2. *Leading with Cultural Intelligence: The Real Secret to Success*, by David Livermore and Soon Ang

## Two Excellent Websites on Culture I Recommend

https://www.geert-hofstede.com/

Geert Hofstede has made it his life's work to understand culture and he has created a set of cultural dimensions to explain and contrast different cultures. I particularly recommend reading his views on the "Power Distance" dimension. Go to the Cultural Tools section on his website and select "Country Comparison". Here you can compare different countries across the cultural dimensions.


http://www.commisceo-global.com/country-guides

Commisceo's free Country Guides and Management Guides are very informative. The Country Guides cover language, culture and etiquette, whereas their Management Guides cover culture from a management perspective. They also have a very good Cultural Awareness Manual which you can download (free) and share with your teams. Finally, you can use their free Quizzes as a team building exercise with your team. For purchase are Country Insight Reports, and they also offer training and consultancy.

## CHAPTER SUMMARY

1. If you lead an international team, have discussions with them about what it means to be respectful, specific, flexible and professional in the context of different cultures.

2. If you have not done so already, brush up your knowledge about culture – there are a wealth of resources at your disposal without trying too hard to find them.

3. Geert Hofstede's website is a good one to understand his cultural dimensions and to find other useful resources. Commisceo has useful country guides and other resources to help brush up your cultural knowledge about specific countries.

oooOooo

# 8| Virtual Communication - Key Considerations

*"The meaning of your communication is the response you get."*
-Milton Erickson

Out of all the challenges in distributed teams, effective communication remains the most challenging. We know that we can get so much more from face-to-face interaction, but that is often not possible with modern teams, where most of our communication relies on a variety of communication technologies.

Miscommunication, delayed response times and misunderstanding are common. This leads not only to frustration, but ineffective work processes and deadline delays.

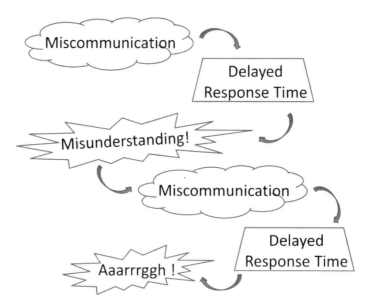

In this chapter, I cover three important considerations that impact virtual communication effectiveness. In subsequent chapters I will share with you some tools and best practices for virtual communication effectiveness.

## Three Key Elements of a Communicated Message

When you communicate a message face-to-face, your total communication is made up of (i)the words you choose, (ii)the way you speak or sound and (iii) the way you look, through your body language.

You probably know that the words you choose form the smallest part of the total interpreted message. The chart below shows the elements of a communicated message, and is often cited by psychologists, and Neuro-Linguistic Programming Practitioners. It is sometimes called the "7-38-55 rule of communication". It was initially proposed by Psychologist Albert Mehrabian in 1967 and is now generally regarded as a reasonably acceptable representation of how our communication is interpreted.

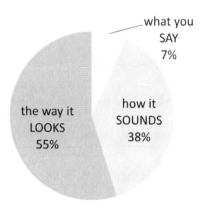

Essentially, in a face-to-face communicated message, the smallest part of the meaning is conveyed through the words chosen. More meaning is added when we can hear the words spoken and of course the greatest meaning is added when we observe the body language.

For example, let's say Bob sends an email to Anna with the words:

*"Despite all the issues, you seem convinced that the project will be delivered on time. Let's discuss this at our meeting tomorrow."*

Anna replies: *"I did not say the project would be delivered on time."*

Those words represent the 7% - the smallest part of the intended message.

However, if this conversation was on the telephone and Anna replied to Bob *"I did not say the project would be delivered on time."*

Her voice emphasis on the word "I" has added to the meaning.

She may have said *"I did not say the **project** would be delivered on time."*

This also has a different meaning to: *"I did not say the project would be delivered on **time**."*

So hearing a person speak the words chosen adds much more to intended meaning and interpreted meaning.

Now, most of our virtual communication is through email, telephone, web meetings and perhaps video conferences. What is the implication of the chart when we communicate with someone we cannot see ?  If I'm hosting a virtual meeting through a video conference, then at least I have the benefit of seeing more information (body language) regarding the intended meaning of the speaker.  On a telephone conference, I am losing a large part of the message, as I can hear but cannot see the person.  Of course in an email, there is a great risk of misinterpretation because text-only messages do not convey intonation and body language.

One of the key considerations for virtual communication is to understand the three elements of a communicated message and to consider how your message will be interpreted through the channel you choose.  Of course, communication is more complex than the 7-38-55 rule.  So now let's explore the concept of "Perceptual Filters" which also affects communication effectiveness.

## Perceptual Filters

Think for a moment how easily we establish firm ideas about people and situations.

For example, what do people say about oil companies? Some people would say that oil companies do not care about the environment.  Others would say that oil companies have a long term commitment to environment preservation and researching alternative forms of energy. What do people say about Accountants?  Some would say they are dull and boring.  Others would say they are smart and interesting.

One of the first things we learn about the world is that not everyone shares our point of view... but your *perception* is *your reality*.  Our perception of a person or situation forms our reality for us, and each of us could have a slightly – or vastly - different perception of the same situation. This is because we all have a unique set of perceptual filters.

Perceptual filters are those aspects of our personality and thought processes that filter our experience of a situation to create our reality. Examples of perceptual filters are our values, attitudes and biases, our current emotions, past experiences, our current expectations of a person or situation and our language ability.

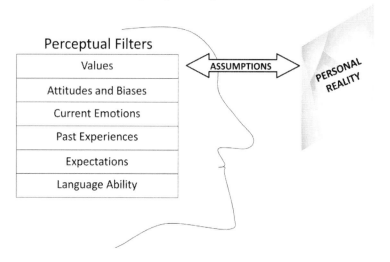

This is why two people can watch exactly the same film at exactly the same time in exactly the same location, and have completely different views of the film. They each have a unique set of perceptual filters.

Perceptual Filters often cause us to assume things that are not necessarily correct, which can result in significant consequences. The NASA communication disaster comes to mind...

In 1999, NASA sent a Mars Climate Orbiter into space. As the spacecraft neared its destination, the engineers at NASA's Jet Propulsion Laboratory who were guiding the Orbiter thought everything was on target. Then, when the craft made its final manoeuvres to enter orbit, they lost communications. Something was terribly wrong.

By examining data from the previous eight hours of the Orbiter's journey, NASA realized that the craft's approach had been much lower than intended – about 60 km above the planet's surface instead of 150 to 180 km. The altered course meant a rough ride through the Martian atmosphere that the Orbiter was not designed to withstand. The following day, the engineers concluded that the spacecraft had not survived the miscalculation, and the search for the Orbiter was abandoned.

The follow-up investigation found that the root cause of the problem was communication between the two teams responsible for the launch.

These virtual teams communicated mainly by e-mail, but failed to realise that the team in Colorado was working with metric units and the team in California with Imperial units. Both teams worked with the assumption that what they communicated to the other team was clear. Over US$125m was lost. [If you're interested in getting the full story, search for "NASA disaster 1999" on the internet.]

Another example: I was facilitating a course with an international team. An English participant (Jack) was explaining how overloaded they were, and said his boss "was trying to squeeze blood out of a stone." A participant from Philadelphia (Jane) asked him to confirm what that phrase meant as it didn't makes sense to her. Jack explained that to squeeze blood out of a stone means to push people unreasonably beyond what they are capable of. Jane then said, "Oh yes, we have something similar. We talk about squeezing blood out of a turnip." Lars from Norway looked perplexed and said "What is a turnip ?"

Let's go back to Anna and Bob, who each have a unique set of perceptual filters. If Anna wants to tell Bob that there are some issues on her project, her perceptual filters will affect her choice of words and the way she expresses herself. She will have an <u>expectation</u> of Bob's understanding of the project. She might <u>value</u> openness and honesty, and will raise the issues even if this may result in conflict. She might currently be <u>feeling</u> frustrated, which will affect her tonality and choice of words. Through Bob's set of perceptual filters, he may <u>expect</u> that she doesn't tell him about problems, rather the solutions she has identified. Bob could also currently be extremely busy, and <u>feel</u> frustrated that he does not have time for this. He may also have a <u>view</u> that Anna is young and inexperienced and that she may not know what she is talking about.

Anna communicates with Bob through a channel. This could be face-to-face, on the telephone, a video conference or an email. In the channel, there is also noise. Noise is what distorts the message. There are two types of noise:

The first is External noise – If they were talking on the telephone and it's a bad line, the noise could affect the clarity of the message. The second type of noise is internal noise… this is where most of the noise arises - this is the noise inside our heads. This is the running commentary and other thoughts we all have while other people are communicating with us. The more internal noise we have, the less attention we are paying to the intended message and therefore the greater the risk of the message being distorted.

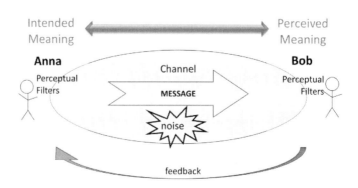

So far, we understand that text-based-only communication, like email, delivers only a small part of the intended message and the misinterpretation risk of an email is higher than a telephone conversation or a video conference.

We also understand that each person has a unique set of perceptual filters. Our perceptual filters will affect the way we communicate a message to others and the way a message is interpreted.

## Media Richness

Media Richness Theory was initially proposed by Daft and Lengel, who proposed:

*"Information richness is defined as the ability of information to reach understanding within a time interval".*

Communication channels that promote understanding in a timely manner are considered more rich. Communication channels that take a longer time to convey understanding are considered less rich.

So does this mean face-to-face, or a video conference, is always best ? Can you think of a situation where understanding will be conveyed quicker through an email, or a telephone call or an instant message?

The key message is that no one channel is better than the other in all situations. They all have their place, depending on the situation, what you want to communicate and who you are communicating with. With an understanding of these key considerations for virtual communication effectiveness, read the next chapter where I used my PLANTT checklist to help you choose the right channel.

## CHAPTER SUMMARY

1. Virtual communication effectiveness remains one of the most challenging aspects of collaborating in a distributed team.

2. The aim of your communication to others is to minimise the gap between your intended message and their interpreted understanding.

3. Three key considerations can affect this: (i)the elements of an intended message (words, sound, body language.) and how this is interpreted based on the channel you choose, (ii)perceptual filters – my perceptual filters will impact how I communicate and others' perceptual filters will impact their interpretation of my message; (iii)media richness theory which implies that face-to-face communication is not always best – the best channel is the one that will reach understanding the quickest.

oooOooo

# 9| Choosing the Right Communication Channels

*"The single biggest problem in communication is the illusion that it has taken place."*
-George Bernard Shaw

**Tools and Templates in this Chapter:**

- PLANTT Communication Checklist

With a host of virtual communication channels to choose from, how do we choose the best channel for each communication scenario? We cannot say richer channels (such as face-to-face or video conference) – are better than leaner channels (such as email or intranet updates). My PLANTT checklist of considerations should help you decide how to "plant the right message" and avoid misunderstanding.

## Asynchronous vs. Synchronous Channels of Communication

Asynchronous channels are channels where the communication is "one-way" and a response is unlikely to be received immediately. Email and posted letters are examples of asynchronous channels.

Synchronous channels are those where dialogue can take place at the same time, even though people are in different places. Telephone calls and audio/video conferences are examples of synchronous channels.

In virtual teams, we quite often see people trying to have dialogue over email. Whilst this is useful in some cases, it is not always ideal as the email can be misinterpreted, and, more importantly, this conversation will take longer. Instant Messaging is an example of a channel which could be synchronous or asynchronous depending on whether both messenger and receiver are virtually present at the same time.

## PLANTT Communication Checklist

My PLANTT checklist is useful to help you consider important aspects that could affect your channel choice and the order in which you determine different channels should be used for the same scenario.

> **P**urpose
> **L**anguage ability
> **A**uditability requirements
> **N**umbers to communicate with
> **T**ime urgency
> **T**ime zone difference

## PLANTT Communication Channel Considerations

| Purpose: | Non-Complex | Partially Complex | Complex | Highly Complex |
|---|---|---|---|---|
| Language Ability: | Good | Average | Poor | Very Poor |
| Auditability Requirements: | Not Required | Partially Required | Required | Rigorously Required |
| Numbers: | 1 person | Small team | Several teams | Entire organisation |
| Time Urgency: | >2 weeks | 1-2 weeks | 1 week | 1 day |
| Time Zone Difference: | 0-1 hour | 2-3 hours | 4-6 hours | >6 hours |

## PURPOSE of the Communication

What is the purpose of your communication? Is it to inform, get buy-in, solve a problem, facilitate a decision or is it part of an ongoing discussion? How complex is the situation?

## LANGUAGE Ability

What is the language ability between you and the person or group you need to communicate with?

## AUDITABILITY Requirements

Do you need to have an audit trail of the communication? Some communication scenarios need to be recorded for legal reasons, or an audit trail may be desirable in case it needs to be referred to later.

**NUMBERS**

How many people are you having to communicate with?

**TIME Urgency**

How urgently do you need to communicate with a person or group? How urgently do you need their response or action?

**TIME Zone Differences**

Where are the people located that you need to communicate with and what is the time zone differences between you?

## PLANTT Communication Examples

Example 1: Performance Problem

Sue is based in London and has a team member, Sergei, based in St Petersburg. Sergei is a Product Manager and has been under-performing over the last three months. Sue is scheduled to visit the St Petersburg office in 4 weeks' time. However, she cannot wait until then to get to the root of the problem. They have a 1:1 meeting by telephone every 2 weeks. He cancelled their last call because he had something urgent to attend to. During their previous call, they discussed his performance and he indicated that he was having problems with people at the manufacturing site, which he was resolving. Their next call is in 3 days' time. This morning Sue received an email from the local Quality Manager at St Pietersburg, raising his concerns about the way Sergei talks to him and his staff at the factory. She uses her PLANTT checklist to help her decide the best channels of communication to use in this situation, and the order in which those channels should be used.

**Sue's PLANTT Considerations…**

Purpose: *To escalate the significance of Sergei's performance problems with him, and agree a plan of resolution.* I decided this is complex because I have raised this with Sergei previously and no improvements have been noted.

Language Ability: We have to communicate in English, and Sergei's English is reasonably poor. He finds it difficult to understand, and make himself understood in English especially verbally. He finds written communication easier to understand.

Auditability Requirements: Given that Sergei's performance is declining, and it does not appear that he has taken any ownership to resolve the problem despite my coaching and advice, an audit trail of communication from here on is required. I do not expect this to escalate to a formal performance management situation, but I want to keep an audit trail just in case.

Numbers: For the moment, this is just between me and Sergei.

Time Urgency: Our next scheduled 1:1 is in three days. It can wait until then. However, I must impress upon Sergei that this is an important call and cannot be rescheduled or cancelled. I cannot move my upcoming St Petersburg trip closer, so this meeting will have to be a virtual meeting.

Time Zone Difference:  It is summer time in the UK, so we have just two hours' time zone difference.  Our call is scheduled for 3pm St Petersburg time.

Given her PLANTT analysis, Sue decides the following:

1. **Email** Sergei this morning outlining the purpose of their meeting in three days' time.  The email should state the performance areas they will discuss and include any preparation he should perform before their meeting.  Advise Sergey to book a room as the meeting will be via WebEx with video and not the usual telephone call.  The email should also stress that this meeting cannot be cancelled or rescheduled as it is a high priority.  Their meeting is 3pm-4pm St Petersburg time.  Also ask Sergei to clear his schedule for the rest of the afternoon in case they need more time.  The subject line of the email is "Important Upcoming 1:1".  Note: Your email subject line is almost as important as the content of the email.  Think about what you put in the subject.

2. **Schedule** the WebEx meeting and call it "Important Upcoming 1:1".

3. Host the **WebEx meeting** with Sergei, **with video** for both switched on.  Include any relevant documents to refer to.  Agree with Sergei what he will do over the coming weeks until Sue's visit, and confirm any support he needs from her.  Ask Sergei to document his understanding of the meeting purpose and action points, and email it to her within 24 hours.

4. Schedule a **weekly WebEx (video on)** with Sergei until her St. Petersburg visit, when she can meet with him and some of the other people at the site.

Most managers agree that performance problems should be resolved face-to-face. However, this is not always immediately possible, as in the above example. The above is an indication of how my PLANTT checklist informed Sue which channels to use, in which order and timing, to resolve this performance problem.

Example 2: Company Split

Sue leads a team of nine Product Managers across seven locations in Europe and Asia. Sergei is one of her Product Managers and she is pleased to advise us that four months later they have overcome his performance problems and he is doing well.

However, the organisation has decided that it is going to split into two core businesses. This is not a surprise as it has been under discussion for some time – most staff are aware of the pending split. Up until now, Sue was only able to tell her team that she would let them know any news as soon as she knew it.

All the managers (Sue included) were officially briefed by the CEO via a Webinar this morning. The Webinar's purpose was to make the split decision official with all managers, to explain how the split would take place and how various business units would be affected. A detailed email was sent by the CEO's office to all staff after the Webinar at 11am UK time today.

Sue's team will be affected, as some will continue to report to her whilst others will report into a newly branded organisation following the split. It is not clear yet whether people will need to move or not. She now needs to meet with her team members to discuss this.

## Sue's PLANTT Considerations...

Purpose: *To explain how the split will affect our team (including timelines), and to answer any questions they have.* This is a highly complex situation because this affects their jobs. The split will only be finalised in seven months' time, and I can expect resistance to change as well as performance problems due to them being worried about the split.

Language Ability: We have to communicate in English, and there are varying levels of ability from good to poor. The detailed email from the CEO's head office was well-written and designed to maximise understanding.

Auditability Requirements: I need to demonstrate that I have briefed my team and given them an opportunity to ask questions and raise concerns. An audit trail is partially required (i.e. this is not my primary focus compared to the previous example where it was more important).

Numbers: Ten people including myself.

Time Urgency: Even though my team was expecting this, the email will have been a shock to some who perhaps were in denial and unsure that the split would actually take place. I would say the time urgency is as soon as possible, within <u>one week</u> of the email that was sent out today.

<u>Time Zone Difference</u>: Seven hours to include my Product Manager in Singapore.

Given the above, Sue decided the following:

1. **Schedule a 90-minute WebEx meeting** with the team for 8am UK time within the next 5 working days. If there is not a time when all can meet, choose a time and advise them that this is a priority and to reschedule any other meeting conflicts. State the purpose of the meeting is to explain in detail how the split will affect our team, and to answer any questions they have. [Note: I would have preferred to schedule a Telepresence meeting, but the Telepresence Room has already been booked out over the next two weeks.]

2. **Send a separate email** referring them to the WebEx meeting invite, stressing it's importance. Ask them to read the CEO's email and to note any questions they have for me as preparation for the meeting. They should email me their questions before the meeting (this will help me gauge level of engagement and level of concern). Advise them we will be turning our video cameras on, and to ensure they have an appropriate space where they can attend the meeting.

3. **Call Lutz** in Germany and ask him to be the note taker of the meeting. This will free me to focus on the meeting. Lutz has a good attention to detail and will not be affected by the split.

4. Host the **WebEx meeting** with everyone to achieve its purpose. Advise them that Lutz will be emailing the meeting notes within 24 hours of the meeting.

5. At the meeting, ask each participant to schedule a **1:1 call with me** within the next week (if we do not have one already) for us to discuss this further.

6. **Ongoing discussions** will be held during our bi-monthly 1:1 meetings and our monthly team meetings.

7. Schedule a **1½ day team face-to-face meeting** within 2 months. The purpose is to discuss the split and plans moving forward.


Thinking through the communication steps and channels in advance is important. For example, if Sue reacted without thinking, and thought it would be better to have 1:1s with each of her team members first... can you imagine how very different the outcome would be?

## CHAPTER SUMMARY

The essence of the PLANTT checklist is not to tick boxes so that it is immediately clear what to do. The main aim of using this checklist is to think before you react; to think more holistically before you do what you normally do, whether your norm is to email or call a meeting. By thinking it through, you are likely to avoid using the wrong channel which leads to misunderstanding and further problems.

oooOooo

## 10| Virtual Meeting Best Practices

*"A meeting is an event in which the minutes
are kept and the hours are lost."*

-Unknown

**Tools and Templates in this Chapter:**

- Meeting Effort-Value Audit
- PASTA Virtual Meeting Checklist

Meetings are a great way to have dialogue instead of mass emails. They are also a great opportunity to build relationships. However, meetings can also be a massive time waster. Asana is a software company that had this very problem – too many meetings to the detriment of meeting project deadlines. So they introduced "No Meeting Wednesdays." I think it's a great idea – an entire day where you can focus on everything but meetings. This may be a bit extreme for some, but you can still apply the spirit of what Asana did: protect some time from meetings, for example "no meetings on Wednesdays between 8am and 11am GMT" if you are working with an EMEA team.

If you find there are too many meetings in your team, use the template below to perform a **meetings audit**.

## Meeting Effort-Value Audit

Complete the table below, showing:

a) The names of the meetings you attend. In brackets indicate who the attendees are.

b) Whether the meeting is planned/scheduled or tends to be ad-hoc.

c) The frequency of these meetings, e.g. weekly, bi-monthly, monthly etc. For ad-hoc meetings, indicate frequency per period, e.g. per quarter.

d) The channel for these meetings: face-to-face, telephone call, audio conference, etc.

e) The relative value of the meeting: high, medium or low.

f) The relative effort involved in preparing for the meeting and attending the meeting: high, medium or low.

| Ref. | Meeting Name/ Description and attendees | Planned/ Ad-Hoc | Frequency | Channel | Value (H/M/L) | Effort (H/M/L) |
|---|---|---|---|---|---|---|
| 1 | | | | | | |
| 2 | | | | | | |
| 3 | | | | | | |
| 4 | | | | | | |
| 5 | | | | | | |

Once you have completed the table, you can plot your meetings on a chart for visual impact:

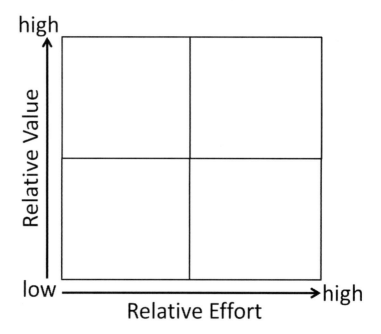

This is a great way to make a case for optimising the meetings you have in your team.

If you are a victim of other people's meetings, and you feel that many of them have low value compared to relative high effort, you should make a case for being removed from the meeting or attending the part that is relevant to you only.


Now let's look at how you can make the most of your virtual meetings. These are best practices if you are the meeting facilitator. You can translate some of these practices if you are the meeting participant and not a facilitator.

## PASTA Checklist for Virtual Meeting Best Practices

Participants

Agenda

Schedule

Technology

After

## Participants

1. Differentiate between Participants and Attendees. You cannot host an interactive meeting with large numbers of people and expect all of them to participate and all of them to stay engaged. The guideline for virtual meeting participant numbers is <u>less than nine</u>. More than eight, and you start losing control of their engagement (whether you are aware of it or not). I was working with a Project Portfolio Manager who thought it was a good idea to host a bi-monthly status meeting with all 16 Project Managers. The meeting was an hour and the intention was for each Project Manager to give a "quick" update on their project status. Do the math and you can figure what went

wrong... by the time they got to Project Manager number 9, they had run out of time. I was sitting with two of the Project Managers at a remote office, and it was also clear that by the time we got to the status of the fourth project, people were losing interest and working on other things. Decide in advanced who needs to participate and who is invited to attend. Attendees have the choice whether they want to attend or not. Participants must attend and prepare for their participation at the meeting.

2. Limit the participation list to less than nine *participants*. If you do not need *participation*, i.e. you are meeting purely to inform a group of people about something, you can have as many (muted) attendees as you wish on the call/webinar.

3. Assign attendance roles if these roles are not obvious: Facilitator, Note Taker, Participant, Non-Participating Attendee.

4. If you are hosting a team meeting as their manager, it is a good idea to rotate the meeting Facilitator and Note Taker. I mentioned this once on a course and one of the participants was horrified as this would diminish his authority as the manager. This is not the case. You still retain authority as you are their boss and you have openly declared to the team that you are delegating meeting facilitation responsibilities. The reason is for rotating the Facilitator role is for team members to practice virtual meeting facilitation. This is good for their career development. This also frees you up to focus on what is being said during the meeting rather than on controlling the meeting dynamics, sticking to the agenda and managing within the

allocated time. Rotating Note Taker is also a good idea as it shares the administrative responsibility. It also gives you immediate feedback about how well individuals in your team have understood the key points from the meeting.

5. To maximise engagement, structure the meeting participation so that no one person speaks for more than three minutes (including yourself). This vocal variety keeps people's attention. Even if you speak with vocal variety yourself, after three minutes it becomes boring and sounds the same.

6. Participants are people. People have names. Use their names when facilitating participation. Asking open questions like "So what do you all think about the proposal?" or "Does anyone have any questions?" is not going to work. You will either get everyone talking over each other or be met with a wall of silence. You are the voice traffic controller, so ensure you bring people into the conversation by using their name. Using someone's name also brings them back to attention if they wandered off. I'm certain you would have had the experience walking down the street when someone calls your name. You are immediately brought to attention, whether they were actually calling you or not.

## Agenda

7. Publish a focused Agenda that shows time allocation for each topic and who will lead on that topic.

8. Allow time in your Agenda for people to introduce themselves if they have not met previously.

9. Hold some time in reserve to summarise actions and ask for each participant's final contribution.

## Schedule

10. Consider time zones and people's personal time when choosing the time for the meeting. I was working with a team in Singapore and we were talking about this. One of the team told me she had to attend a weekly meeting at 7pm on a Friday night. The idea of the meeting was to recap on project progress during the week and to set the priorities for the following week. However, it transpired that the meeting only included participants from Europe and Asia. There was no need for it to be so late. I encouraged her to ask for the meeting to be made earlier, as their meeting host was probably naïve to the inconvenience this was causing.

11. Limit the duration of meetings. Here are some best practice guidelines, depending on the meeting tool:

  - Tele-conferences: 30 minutes ideal; 45 minutes OK, 1 hour maximum.
  - Web meetings (like WebEx, Skype etc.): 60 to 90 minutes.
  - Video-conferences and telepresence meetings: max 2 hours.
  - If you need longer sessions, allow a 10 minute break every hour.

## Technology

12. Ensure everyone on your team is trained to use the meeting tools. If they are attending tele-conferences, ensure they know where to obtain the access call numbers. If they are attending web meetings, ensure they know how to use the many tools provided with the technology.

13. Encourage use of tele-presence or video conferences if you have access to these technologies. If you have tele-presence, respect that many people will want to use this tool as a replacement for face-to-face meetings, so keep your meeting duration to a respectful minimum.

14. To maximise engagement, use the functionality provided with web meeting tools.

## After

15. Publish meeting decisions and actions with responsibilities and deadlines.

16. Build in a practice for yourself and with your team that meeting notes should be published within 24 hours of the meeting.

17. If you are using a web meeting tool and have allocated responsibility for someone to take notes, they can write up the meeting decisions and actions "live" during the meeting for all to see on a virtual whiteboard.

## CHAPTER SUMMARY

1. Meetings are a great way to have dialogue instead of mass emails. They are also a great opportunity to build relationships. Meetings can also be a massive time waster.
2. Use my Meeting Effort-Value Audit tool to assess and optimise your team meetings.
3. Apply the PASTA best practices to get the most out of your virtual meetings.

oooOooo

# 11| Email Best Practices

*"Email is familiar. It's comfortable. It's easy to use. But it might just be the biggest killer of time and productivity today."*

-Ryan Holmes

**Tools and Templates in this Chapter:**

- CARE Email Checklist
- Email Protocol Example

I remember when email became a reality at my first job in the 1990's. It was so exciting. Such a great way to communicate quickly rather than rely on letters which are now affectionately called "snail mail." People have built relationships and destroyed relationships on email. They have solved problems and created problems. They have owned and communicated decisions, and have passed the buck to a wide distribution list where accountability is diluted. Most organisations today suffer from Email Cholesterol due to bad email habits. In this chapter, I share with you my CARE checklist which is a quick and easy way to check our emails before sending them. People have also asked me to send them "email best practices", so I have included an Email Protocol which you can tailor to your team as necessary.

## CARE Email Checklist

Send emails with CARE. Before clicking the "send" button, check:

1. **C**lear: Is my email clear? Does the Subject fit the content? Have I kept it as short and unambiguous as possible? When I read it as if I was the recipient, is it clear what is expected of me once I have read the email?

2. **A**ccurate: Is it accurate? Have I accurately reflected the people in the "To" and "CC" fields. Those that must take action should be in the "To" field. If I have referred to data, dates or times, are these accurate? If you have referred to an attachment, is it actually attached ?

3. **R**espectful: Have I respectfully addressed the email to the person/people correctly? Some people prefer "Dear Mr Schultz", whilst other are OK with "Hi Wolfgang". What is the tone of my email ? Is it respectful to the person/people I am sending it to ? Part of being respectful is not sending an email to people (or cc'ing people) unless they must see the email. If I am asking for something to be done by a deadline date, have I respectfully taken their workload into consideration?

4. **E**ngaging: Does the subject line make people want to open the email, ignore it or delete it? Is the content worth reading? How do you *feel* when you read the

email from the recipient's perspective? Is your intent best served by an email or a telephone call ?

The above seems like a lot to check. First check all fields (To, CC, Subject, Attachments, Content, Footer). Then do a quick check for Clear, Accurate, Respectful and Engaging. This check should take you no longer than 1-2 minutes (unless you end up making major changes) and could prevent problems due to carelessness.

Have a look at the three emails below which form an audit trail, and decide whether they are clear, accurate, respectful and engaging…

## Email Examples

### Email Example 1

**From:** Nick Franks
**Sent:** Friday, November 4, 2016 13:52 PM
**To:** Jan de Beer
**Subject:** Re: Proposal Feedback
**Attachments:** Proposal Comments

Dear Jan

Thank you for the great work you did on the proposal.

I have gone through it all and have made some comments summarised in the attached document. As you know, the client needs this by next Friday, November 11$^{th}$. Please have my comments integrated by next Wednesday, November 9$^{th}$, so that I can check and forward on to the Client by Friday.

Have a great weekend!

Regards,

Nick

### Email Example 2

**From:** Jan de Beer
**Sent:** Friday, November 4, 2016 13:53 PM
**To:** Nick Franks
**Subject:** Out of Office: Proposal Feedback

Thank you for your email.
I am on vacation until the 20$^{th}$ with no access to emails.

Jan

## Email Example 3

**From:** Nick Franks
**Sent:** Monday, November 7th, 2016 10:45 PM
**To:** Jan de Beer
**Cc:** Tomas, Kirk, Elke, Antonio, Sebastian, Jean, Shahzeb, Mustafa, Timo, Tina, Franco
**Subject:** Out of Office: Proposal Feedback

Dear Jan

I have left messages on your voicemail all day and sent you an sms. I have also sent you a further three emails to your personal email account. I know you say that you have no access to emails but Elke said that the hotel you are staying at on vacation has got free wifi, so you should pick this up.

Your Out of Office does not leave a contact number or someone else that can help me in your absence. I couldn't find anyone in your department that was able to make the changes, so I will have to make them myself. However, I cannot be certain that my changes are accurate – you need to check this before I finalise it and send it to the Client on Friday, as some of this stuff is your speciality. Either check it or update it from where you are; or let me know how you would like to proceed. Or perhaps make someone else available that can support me on this. Do you have someone I can contact? Also who was your main contact at the Client when you discussed the technical details? There seems to be quite a lot of information missing. Otherwise I am going to send it off as is. This is quite stressful for me, as I am now working late at night!

If you don't reply to this on time, you will have to take responsibility if we lose the contract because the proposal is incorrect. I am doing the best I can from my side. I will lose a lot of time updating it, which was what you should have done.

Nick

*Let us all sharpen up and use email properly.*

If you have email usage problems in your organisation or in your teams, then perhaps create an Email Protocol or Email Usage Policy, and ensure people are reminded of how to use email to best effect.

## Email Protocol Example

### Email Header
1. Only mark your message as high priority when it truly is.
2. The "To:" field is for those you want a response from or those that must take action.

3. The "Cc:" field is for those you want to keep in the loop because they need to know. Only include someone on the Cc: field if the person is involved with the topic and you are certain they need to know.

4. Make subject lines clear and specific. This helps readers know quickly what the email is about. If it is an actionable item with a deadline, include that in the subject line.

5. Extend the same courtesy when issuing calendar invitations, which should include a clear subject line.

6. If you tag onto an older email, update the subject line so it reflects the new subject matter – and delete any subject matter that is no longer needed to keep the email trail clean and succinct.

7. Never send a message with the subject line left blank.

8. Use a separator (|) in the Subject Line to indicate the purpose of the email, for example: "Draft Proposal | Action Required"; or "2020 Blueprint | For Information".

## Email Content

9. Make the email easy to read. Use font sizes of at least 10 pts. A font size of 12 pts is commonly used for business. Standard fonts in black are preferred.

10. Get to the point in the opening sentences.

11. Write short sentences and short paragraphs. They are faster and easier to read than long ones.

12. Keep the email as short and focused as possible. If an email must be long, consider breaking it up into sections with headers or bullets.

13. Remember that email is not private. Choose your words carefully because email never goes away. Keep

this in mind, especially when the topic is sensitive, emotional, or controversial.

14. Bear in mind that your work email is considered property of the organisation and can be forwarded and retrieved even after it has been deleted.

## Email Footer

15. Include an email signature. Many organisations have a standard policy and presentation of email signatures. However, if you do not have one, be sure to create one and include your full name and contact information.

## Replying to Email

16. Only "reply to all" if it is essential that all recipients see the response.

17. Respond to emails promptly and reply with complete responses. If you're answering someone's questions, consider numbering or bulleting your responses to make your email easy to follow.

18. If you cannot reply in full in a timely manner, let the sender know when they can expect a full reply from you.

19. If the answer(s) is too complex for email, schedule a meeting with the individual(s).

20. Review all new emails before sending off responses. There may have been an email trail which has solved the problem and no longer needs your input.

21. Ensure you have activated the automatic spell-check option for your emails.

22. Ensure all attachments are indeed attached. [Note: I have built a habit that serves me well after too many reply emails saying "Thank you for your email

Emanuela, but there is no attachment." Now, every time I write the word "attached" I stop typing and check that the attachment is there and if not, attach it before finishing my sentence. My CARE checklist helps with this as well.}

23. Be aware of your virtual tone. Remember that the recipient of your email can't see or hear you. Check that your tone won't be perceived as aggressive or offensive. Avoid writing with all capitals or an unusually large font size, as it may be perceived that you are shouting at the email recipient/s. Do not write in red font.

## Out-of-Office

24. Set an Out-of-Office message when you are unavailable. Alert others to your absence with an automatic note so they aren't waiting for a response from you. Include information on when you will return and the name of someone who may be able to provide assistance in your absence.

25. Remember to remove the automatic notification when you return to the office. It is frustrating and professionally eyebrow-raising getting an auto-reply on 12th May saying "I am out of the office, back on 9th May."

## Avoid Email Abuse

26. Switch off the "request read receipt" as a default, and only request a read receipt in exceptional cases. The same applies for delivery receipts.

27. Don't hide behind email. Sometimes personal contact is better than email for certain topics.

28. If you are discussing sensitive information or find that you are emailing back and forth for too long, a telephone conversation is better.

29. Don't respond to an email if you are angry or frustrated. It's better to calm down and think things through first. Consider calling the person to discuss the matter rather than sending a reply that you may regret later.

30. Consider other communication channels. Using email too frequently, when not necessary, or sending an email to a large or inappropriate audience is not effective or efficient.

**CHAPTER SUMMARY**

1. Email has its rightful place as a communication and collaboration enabler for virtual teams.

2. Use my CARE checklist for a quick and easy way to check your emails before sending them.

3. If email is abused in your organisation or team, create and distribute an Email Protocol (or Email Usage Policy). Be sure to train users on its implementation using video or online web meeting sessions.

oooOooo

# 12| Trust and Team Identity

*"The measure of a good leader is not what you do, but what people do because of you."*

-Howard Hendricks

Having people trust and respect each other in the distributed team is essential, and it all starts with you. First, I will facilitate your self-reflection. Next, I will provide you with some additional tips to build trust between team members and get them to identify with your objectives and/or your team.

## Lessons from Brand Management

Successful global brands have shown us how to build trust and loyalty. What is brand loyalty ? Simply, it is the preference of customers to continue to purchase the same brand of products or services rather than to consider competitor offerings. How do companies achieve this hypnotic state of preference ? It does not happen overnight. When I host workshops and ask the question "What do organisations do to build brand loyalty?", this is typically what ends up on the flip chart:

- The product/s or service/s under the brand are consistently **reliable.**

- The brand is **credible** – we believe what they promise because we have witnesses their track record of success.

- The organisation demonstrates an **interest** in its customers by becoming customer-intimate: they know about customer needs, difficulties and aspirations.

- The product/s or service/s under the brand are easily **available** when required.

- People personally **identify** with the brand: the brand demonstrates **similar values** to what its customers have.

The above is not a complete list. People also make notes about testimonies and association, etc. It is at this point we can stop working on the list and translate the learning...

*In a nutshell, people need to have consistent positive experiences of the brand to build their trust in the brand. When this trust is consistently perceived, loyalty sets in.*

I asked a brand expert to explain to me the difference between a "product" and a "brand", and he told me that *the brand is the personality of the product*. Think about the iPhone: the product is a smart phone. Think about Manchester United: the product is a football club. The brand represents values and behaviours just like people have behaviours which are a function of their values. People that are brand loyal to the iPhone or to Manchester United have an emotional connection with those brands (whether they are aware of it or not).

So, what does this mean for you – the distance manager or remote leader ?  Your Job Title is the product.  Project Manager, or VP EMEA Sales, or Head of R&D.  Your *name* AND *how people identify with you when they interact with you is the brand.*

- If you want people to identity with your objectives and priorities, *they must identify with YOU.*

- For people to identify with you, *they must feel a connection with you.*

- For people to feel a connection with you, *they must have consistent positive experiences of you.*

### *So here is your self-reflection question:*

*What experiences do people have when interacting with you?  How do they experience your virtual personality?*

With the above as foundation work, you can extend this concept to the team.  The diagram below reflects an example of key behaviours (inside the triangle) and values (outside the triangle) a distance manager would expect team members to model.

We all practice:

**REALIABILITY**
by doing what we say

**CREDIBILITY**
through demonstrated success

**INTEREST**
in each other

**AVAILABILITY**
to each other

We Value Dialogue

We Value Ownership

We Value Openness

## Tips to Nurture Trust and Team Identity

1.  Hire people you can trust, then trust the people you hire. Most people really want to do a great job as best they can. Trust them to do so, and manage performance problems swiftly.

2.  As a team building exercise, get your team to come up with their own ingredients in the "team glue". Design the model and have it visible during relevant virtual team meetings.

3.  Do not break trust by not practicing what you preach. This has been said so many times, but it is essential to lead by example.

4.  Get team members to experience each other's work places if possible. Start up a site visit programme or job swap. For example, Jose in Lisbon could swap with Antoine in Paris for a week. Alternatively, Jose

could visit Antoine for two days and shadow him to understand how work is carried out there. Be sure to consult with your team as some of them may have a personal life that does not allow them to be away from home.

5. Encourage the use of Instant Messaging (IM). This technology replaces the "water cooler" meetings. Send an IM to team members just to say "hi" or ask them about their weekend. They can also use IM to quickly check if their team member is available for an unscheduled phone call about a work related matter. IM is not only great for relationship building, but creates greater access to team members on their terms. As a result, it is a great productivity booster.

6. Meet face-to-face at least once a year. The ideal would be quarterly. It would be good to meet twice a year. When you do get together in a co-located environment, it is a *golden opportunity to reinforce the glue that binds the team*. PLEASE do not waste their time by requiring them to listen to presentation after presentation of graphs and performance figures and visioning and strategising and… yaaaawwwn. Use the opportunity to collectively identify opportunities for improvement, to perhaps have some training, and most importantly to enjoy fun team building exercises. See next Chapter for more insights about how you should harness your face-to-face meetings.

## CHAPTER SUMMARY

1. Trust is essential in all teams, but purposefully building trust and team identity in distributed teams is even more essential as remote team members lack the ad-hoc social interactions that co-located teams enjoy.

2. Building trust and a sense of team identity starts with you – the remote leader. Self-assess how people experience you, and work on building consistent positive experiences. The key behaviours to model are credibility, reliability, interest in others and availability to them. The glue that binds trust in the team are core values like valuing openness, dialogue and each person taking ownership.

3. Trust and identity in the team, or identity with you and your objectives, needs to be constantly reinforced.

4. Use face-to-face interactions as a golden opportunity to nurture and nourish relationships through fun team building experiences.

oooOooo

# 13| Face-to-Face Golden Opportunities

*"The best way to predict your future is to create it."*

-Peter F. Drucker

Getting together face-to-face with your team is essential for strengthening intra-team relationships and team identity, problem solving, fostering team working culture, and energising team members. If done correctly, remote workers find the event motivational and a form of reward and recognition. In this chapter I summarise my recommendations for planning the event, facilitating the event and following-up after the event.

## Pre-Meeting Actions

Proper planning and preparation is important to ensure that the organisation's spend on the event is realised through a return on the investment, and that the event participants feel their time away from home was well spent. Below are some considerations for pre-meeting planning and preparation:

- Evaluate effectiveness and cost-benefit of previous meeting - factor in adjustments if necessary.
- How big is the team ? Is a team of 200 really a team? Consider whether the entire division/department needs to attend a team event or whether team events should be smaller in size.
- Create a results-focused, structured agenda.
- Include time for fun activities, awards and recognition.

- Research and secure dates and location.
- Rotate and vary meeting location.
- Rotate responsibility for organising meetings.
- Factor in all expenses in the budget.
- Factor considerations relating to cultural sensitivities, personal sensitivities, language ability, and health & safety considerations.
- Circulate agenda to all participants and others that need to be aware of the event agenda.
- Remind participants of pre-meeting activities: e.g. read an article, prepare a presentation, read a briefing on a current business challenge, perform research, complete a Personality Profile, etc. Pre-meeting activities should not take more than one to two hours of participant's time.
- Advise participants of how expenses need to be dealt with in getting to and from the venue and at the venue.

## Team Meeting Activities

### 1.Beginning

- Introduction & Welcome
- Begin with the End in mind - state the goals and set the scene for the day/s ahead

### 2.Middle

The types of activities below should be mixed to create a focused but interactive schedule of events that will keep participants engaged.

Team Building Activities

- Structured fun activities for team building, interaction and learning.
- 1-2 hours per activity; two-three activities per full day.
- Where relevant, summarise learning points from activities and relate these back to workplace scenarios.

Business Challenges

- Participants can create a list of important challenges that need resolving on focused subject matter (do not keep it too broad)
- Solutionising - Focused groups to engineer solutions to the challenges. Solutions should be practical and actionable. Avoid actions like 'improve communication across the regions'. This is too broad - be specific about exactly what needs to be done, by whom and by when.

Learning

- Depending on duration of the off-site event, allocate about 1-2 hours per day for knowledge and skills training on a focused subject matter.
- This can be done by one of the participants or an external consultant.

**3.End**

Action Planning

- Action plans should be practical and implementable.
- Challenge them:

  "What is the impact if this action is not implemented in the desired timeframe ?"

"How will we ensure that this action does in fact take place ?"

- Designate an Action Plan Owner - someone that will take responsibility for updating status against the actions.
- End with the Beginning in mind - summarise and discuss next steps

## Post-Meeting Actions

Within a week: Action Plan Owner to schedule actions according to the agreed plan. Also send out a Survey to get participant feedback about the event.

Within a month: Review the total meeting cost against budget and evaluate cost-benefit

Two months later: formal check on Action Plan status

Four months later: Designate responsibility for next off-site (assuming one every six months or once a year).

TIP: Fun team building experiences do not imply big budget activities. Contact me if I can help you facilitate a structured team building event focused on a theme or specific learning and experience objectives.

## CHAPTER SUMMARY

1. Meeting face-to-face is expensive but a great opportunity to strengthen intra-team relationships and team identity, solve problems, foster team working culture, and energise team members.

2. Spend time in proper preparation to get the most from your investment in time and money.

3. Don't waste the time going through boring presentations which no one is interested in. Plan the event to keep it fun, relevant and purposeful.

4. Follow-up for continuity from the event and to enforce continuous improvement of future events.

oooOooo

# 14| Recruiting the Ideal Remote Worker

*"Strategy without tactics is the slowest route to victory. Tactics without strategy is the noise before the defeat."*

-Sun Tzu

 **Tools and Templates in this Chapter:**

-Checklist: Attributes of the Ideal Remote Team Member

-Remote Team Member Interview Sheet

I have saved this chapter for the end as most people I coach and train on the subject matter of leading remote teams have existing teams that they have either created or inherited. If there comes a time when you get to recruit someone to your team, you should rub your hands with glee at this luxury. Not like when you found some money under the sofa and spontaneously go and purchase something without too much thought. When there is budget for hiring, think very clearly about the ideal remote worker and write up a proper job specification. I am still amazed today when I see organisation's hiring for job functions where clearly the person will be operating remotely from their manager: the job spec focuses on the technical aspects of the job the degrees and certificates that would be beneficial without clearly stating the requirements for being successful as a remote or virtual contributor. In this chapter I share with you my Checklist describing what I think are the attributes of the ideal remote worker (regardless of technical area and job function). I have also created an Interview Form which you can use or modify to help you during the interview process.

## Attributes of the Ideal Remote Team Member

This is not a complete list, and not an ordered list. It is a reminder checklist for you if you have the luxury of recruiting a new team member. Please include the attributes you need for the person to work more autonomously and competently in the job description, and specifically interview for these attributes.

1. **Takes ownership** – Ownership for finding out what is expected of them, for solving problems, for letting you know when they need you or when there are problems requiring your attention.

2. **Ability to prioritise in a changing environment** – Test their ability to work in an ambiguous environment where objectives are not always clear and priorities change. They need to have a mature tolerance of change and ambiguity and able to prioritise their work in these environments.

3. **Ability to manage the environment of distractions in a matrix organisation** – If they will have multiple reporting lines, the best person to manage this dynamic is themselves. Find out how they will manage their managers and their workload for people that have conflicting demands.

4. **Proactive and reactive** – It's not only about being proactive, sometimes people need to react fast by taking appropriate action in a manner that mitigates risk. You may be several time zones away, and will rely on them to take the action needed without waiting for you to wake up or call you at 2am.

5. **Able to work in an international team** – This requires them to enjoy working with mixed cultures and having an ability to adapt their style to different cultures and personalities (if they will be working in an international team).

6. **Self-motivated** – Ideally you want someone that does not need a lot of recognition and appreciation from you, or for you to constantly mobilise them into action. The ideal remote team member is someone that self-motivates.

7. **Good virtual communicator** – The person does not need to have the best language ability and articulation. A good communicator is able to make themselves understood via different communication channels. However, I would definitely test their email writing ability. Most virtual communication is via email, so ensure that the person you have the luxury of selecting can write good emails.

8. **English language skills** – If English is your organisation's international language and most communication will be in English, then this is a must.

9. **Technology skills** – Because technology is the primary means of communication for distributed teams, your ideal candidate should be proficient with the use of common communication and collaboration technologies. They should also be self-sufficient in basic first line technology support.

10. **Comfortable with the travel requirements of the job** – Be clear on how much they will be travelling and check that this is manageable for them.

## Remote Team Member Interview Sheet

My aim is to show you how the job specification criteria specific to remote workers can be translated into an evaluation form during interviews. I cannot stress enough how important it is to include remote-working-specific criteria on job specifications and to specifically interview for these requirements.

## Remote Team Member Interview Sheet

| Interviewee: | Position Applying for: |
|---|---|
| Interviewer/s: | Date: |

**Assessment Scale:**
0 = not demonstrated at all; 1 = partially demonstrated; 2 = generally| demonstrated; 3 = largely demonstrated; 4 = fully demonstrated

1. Demonstrates an ability to take ownership in relevant situations.
   Assessment: 0    1    2    3    4

2. Demonstrates an ability to prioritise in a changing environment.
   Assessment: 0    1    2    3    4

3. Demonstrates an ability to manage typical distractions in a matrix organisation.
   Assessment: 0    1    2    3    4

4. Demonstrates an ability to be proactive and reactive as required.
   Assessment: 0    1    2    3    4

5. Demonstrates an ability to work well with mixed cultures and language abilities.
   Assessment: 0    1    2    3    4

6. Demonstrates an ability to self-motivate.
   Assessment: 0    1    2    3    4

7. Demonstrates an ability to be a good virtual communicator.
   Assessment: 0    1    2    3    4

8. Demonstrates good English language skills.
   Assessment: 0    1    2    3    4

9. Demonstrates an ability to be reasonably technically proficient.
   Assessment: 0    1    2    3    4

10. Demonstrates satisfaction with the travel requirements of the job.
    Assessment: 0    1    2    3    4

## CHAPTER SUMMARY

1. Do not make the mistake of recruiting new remote team members without specifying the skills and qualities needed from someone that will be operating in a virtual team and/or remotely from their manager.

2. Develop a checklist of attributes and convert that to an Interview Sheet to help you find the right person for the job.

3. Ensure you test for the relevant skills and qualities. For example, get them to prepare a presentation that they will need to deliver through a web meeting. Test how they handle technical problems and evaluate the extent to which the candidate can take ownership and need minimal management.

oooOooo

# 15| Six Foundations of Effective Virtual Teams

*"Nail the basics first, detail the details later."*

-Chris Anderson

Some of my clients have asked me for a "quick best practice checklist" that shows the essential requirements for effective virtual teams. I identified 6 key foundations, and this is what I now base my related training courses around.

1. Clarification: Ensuring relevant people are clear on objectives, requirements and expectations.

2. Commitment: Getting alignment and buy-in to your objectives and priorities and delivering to deadlines accordingly.

3. Collaboration: Getting remote colleagues to support you and each other to achieve objectives, despite different priorities, cultures and personality styles.

4. Community: Having a sense of comradery and strong relationships with remote colleagues.

5. Control: Knowing status at any time and having a sense of feeling in control of tasks performed remotely.

6. Communication: Being able to communicate using different channels in a manner that is efficient, maximises understanding and engagement, and facilitates achievement of objectives.

## Practical Application of the 6 Foundations

## An Example

One of my clients is a global financial services organisation. As with many large organisations, over time the organisation becomes over-burdened with inefficient processes and procedures. They initiated a Global Simplification Programme and decided to enable this change through team members that had a strong desire to be part of the solution. An email went out to all staff, contextualising the programme and how it would be supported by top management. They called for applications for a Simplification Ambassador role. The Simplification Ambassadors would be given the equivalent of one working day per week to work on the Simplification Programme. Furthermore, they would be expected to set themselves up as a self-directed virtual team.

The feedback was overwhelmingly positive, and executive management had quite a job to make their final selection of 30 Simplification Ambassadors, representing the business across the globe.

They then brought me in to provide support to the Simplification Ambassadors. Following the Programme kick-off, I suggested the group nominate 8 Simplification Ambassador Representatives (SARs). These representatives would represent the Ambassadors in their region and would be responsible for setting up the team structure and ways of working. I meet with the SARs over several virtual meetings (we used GoToMeeting), and together we carved out a structure and process using the 6 Foundations of Effective Virtual Teams as a framework.

I also created a checklist for them to get clarity around how they will be organised. Some of the items are directive actions, whilst some are questions they need to answer as a group. Below is an excerpt, which you could use as a template for similar project or programmes.

## Simplification Programme Checklist

### Clarification

- Clarify, agree and write up the Objectives and Scope of the Simplification Programme. Also note key Constraints and any key Assumptions.

- Clarify, agree and write up the responsibilities of the Simplification Ambassadors.

- Clarify, agree and write up the responsibilities of the Simplification Ambassador Representatives.

- Agree whether the Representatives chosen will remain for the year, or whether will you be rotating the role, say quarterly.

- Clarify and write-up key Stakeholder expectations with regards to frequency of status updates and reporting format.

## Commitment

- How will you individually maintain high levels of commitment to the programme given your other work priorities?

- How will you maintain commitment with the broader Simplification community?

## Collaboration

- How you will collaborate on cross-function and cross-region initiatives?

- What would be the process for decision making, prioritization, arbitration and escalation if/when required?

- What virtual collaboration tools will you use, and does everyone have access to these tools?

- Create a Code of Collaboration covering team agreements on how email, telephone, GoToMeeting and Instant Messaging should be used.

## Community

- How will you ensure that all the Simplification Ambassadors are treated inclusively and feel like an equal shareholder of this community?

- What is the format and frequency of scheduled interactions between Ambassadors?

## Control

- How will you track and control the simplification initiatives to ensure they are implemented, and improvements are evidenced?

- How will you share best practice, what works and what does not, within the Ambassador community?

- How will you keep the community's efforts visible? For example, will you have a Simplification Intranet page or virtual Kanban-boards showing all initiatives and progress?

- How often will you provide formal status updates to key Stakeholders and the broader organisation community? Through what channels?

- What will status reports look like and who specifically will be consolidating reports?

- How will you ensure everything is documented in case one or more of you becomes unexpectedly unavailable?

## Communication

- What shortlist of communication channels/platforms will you be using? Have you confirmed that everyone has the same access to these across all regions?

- Prepare a Communication Plan for Year 1.

In addition to the above guidance, I also delivered training on "How to Collaborate as an Effective Virtual Team." This training, combined with the guidance on how to set themselves up and get the programme moving, took about four months from kick-off.

They had some teething problems initially, but I would say within 6 months of kick-off they were working exceptionally well as a self-directed virtual team.

**CHAPTER SUMMARY**

1. It is essential for all virtual teams to have the basic foundations in place to work well together.

2. The six foundations I believe are essential pertain to Clarification, Commitment, Collaboration, Community, Control and Communication.

3. These foundations do overlap but can be used as a checklist to help set up your teams for success.

4. Real world application of these foundations has help speed up programmes and give teams what they need to work as a highly effective virtual team.

oooOooo

# APPENDIX

# A1: Popular Software Tools for Virtual Collaboration

I am including this Appendix as people often ask me what are the most popular tools used by companies for virtual collaboration. The risk is that this Appendix will be out of date in six months as the pace of technology innovation is rapidly evolving. My research was conducted between February and June 2017. If you are reading this book any time from January 2018 onwards, perhaps back this up with a quick search of your own.

## Meeting Tools

Skype for Business (used to be Lync)
WebEx
Google Hangouts
GoToMeeting
iMeet
JoinMe
Anymeeting
MeetingBurner

## High-End Video Conferencing Tools

Cisco Telepresence
Polycom Telepresence
Logitech LifeSize

## Instant Messaging Tools

Skype for Business
Yammer (social network owned by Microsoft)
Google Talk
WhatsApp
Jive (social network and related tools)
Sametime
HipChat (Atlassian)

## Document Storage/ File Sharing Tools

SharePoint
Dropbox
Google Drive
Confluence (Atlassian)
Box
Onehub
Zoho Docs

## Project Workflow and Collaboration Tools

Slack
Trello
Jira (Atlassian)
KanbanFlow
Conceptboard
Google Docs (part of Drive)
Scribblar

# A2: Getting in Touch

If you would like to get in touch with me regarding training, coaching or consulting, please email me at emanuela@aikaizen.com.

You can connect with me on LinkedIn here: https://www.linkedin.com/in/aikaizen

## … and a Request

**Please…**

If you found this book useful, please take 2 minutes to complete a short review of the book on your purchase platform.  Authors depend so much on reviews, as do readers who need to decide whether to purchase the book or not.

Thank you in advance, and best wishes.

oooOooo

# About the Author: Emanuela Giangregorio

## A multi-disciplinary, multi-industry, multi-national consultant.

I am a performance improvement consultant with over twenty years' practice delivering bespoke business training, coaching, team building and management consulting. I am South African with Italian heritage, based in the UK, and practice internationally.

I help organisations, teams and individuals be better at what they do, leading to greater fulfilment of personal and organisational goals.

I have written and delivered training programmes in generalist and specialist fields, including topics on strategic leadership, project management, change management, virtual collaboration, and personal effectiveness.

I am tenaciously results-focused, and engage individuals and teams with real-world practical experience, energy, enthusiasm and passion for continuous improvement.

oooOooo

Made in United States
North Haven, CT
26 May 2022